MW01245206

Do You Know Who You Are?

Do You Know Who You Are?

Dr. Grell Ferdinand

Copyright © 2012 by Dr. Grell Ferdinand.

Library of Congress Control Number:		2012912828
ISBN:	Hardcover	978-1-4771-4509-8
	Softcover	978-1-4771-4508-1
	Ebook	978-1-4771-4510-4

All rights reserved. No part of this book may be reproduced or transmitted in any form or by any means, electronic or mechanical, including photocopying, recording, or by any information storage and retrieval system, without permission in writing from the copyright owner.

This book was printed in the United States of America.

To order additional copies of this book, contact:
Xlibris Corporation
1-888-795-4274
www.Xlibris.com
Orders@Xlibris.com
119336

CONTENTS

CHAPTER 1

Sheep Can't Make Goats: God Created Man with Divine Characteristics

"Sheep can't make goats," is an expression that is commonly used in the Caribbean. These words indicate that children tend to resemble their parents physically, and children also inherit other characteristics from their parents. Therefore, knowing who our parents are helps us to determine our true identity and to a large extent influences how we behave.

From stories we have heard, children who were nurtured by apes grew up thinking they were apes and acted like apes. With the entrance of sin every human being has suffered spiritual amnesia: we have forgotten who we really are. In most human beings, birth, childhood, adulthood and death follow each other with a prevailing ignorance of the power, authority, creativity, royalty, Divine assets and glory we have inherited from our Divine Heavenly Father.

Genesis 1:25 provides the background and the context for verse 26 which follows. Genesis 1:25 states: *"And God made the beast of the earth after his kind, and everything that creepeth upon the earth after his kind: and God saw that it was good."* Notice the expression, *"after his kind."* There were many different kinds of animals. The offspring of each kind resembled their parents and behaved in similar ways. In verse 26 we read that God also planned to create His own children *"after his kind,"* or with characteristics like Himself: *"And God said, Let us make man in our image, after our likeness: . . ."* Again in verse 27 we read: *"So God created man in his own image, in the image of God created he him: male and female created he them."* We all know that sin entered and changed the way human beings think and behave. The Psalmist, David, expressed the problem of human sinfulness this way, *"Behold, I was shapen in iniquity; and in sin did my mother conceive me."* In addition to the sinful tendencies we have naturally inherited, Satanic adversaries have deliberately conspired to hide from us our Divine origin, our glorious inheritance, the truth about God's forgiveness and His transforming power over lives.

The Gospel versus the Conspiracy to Hide Truth

God sent His gospel message to the world to reveal to human beings their true identity, so they could become receptive and enjoy their rich heavenly assets. The gospel has been given to us to redefine our behavior and improve our lifestyle by means of God's transforming power working from within us. Generally, we are unaware of our potential and the Divine power that has been made available to us. Lack of true knowledge and understanding which the word of God calls darkness (Isaiah 60:2) has enveloped the whole earth. This ignorance of who we are and what we possess is not by accident, but the result of a deliberate plot perpetuated by the enemy, Satan. The conspiracy to keep us in darkness and deprive us of our Divine assets is explained in 2 Corinthians 4:3,4: *"But if our gospel be hid, it is hid to them that are lost; In whom the god of this world hath blinded the minds of them which believe not, lest the light of the glorious gospel of Christ, who is the image of God, should shine unto them."* Thank God that He did not abandon us to live in darkness, but poured out on us the glorious truth of the gospel of Christ. In spite of the conspiracy to keep us in ignorance, light is spreading like wild fire to all parts of the world. Those who have benefited from the light of the gospel can testify like the Apostle Paul:

> *"For I am not ashamed of the gospel of Christ: for it is the power of God unto salvation to every one that believeth; to the Jew first, and also to the Greek. For therein is the righteousness of God revealed from faith to faith: as it is written, THE JUST SHALL LIVE BY FAITH."*

We Are Joint-Heirs with Jesus and Predestined to Become Like Him

The gospel reveals that there are no ordinary human beings on planet earth. We may not know it, but the reality is that our Heavenly Father has empowered and promoted us to an elevated status where He now considers us to be joint-heirs with Jesus. This truth is revealed in Romans 8:16,17: *"The Spirit itself beareth witness with our spirit, that we are the children of*

God: And if children, then heirs; heirs of God, and joint-heirs with Christ; if so be that we suffer with him, that we may be also glorified together."

Moreover, Romans 8:29 (Amplified) informs us that we have a secure and an exalted future. Not only do we share a Divine inheritance, but Our Heavenly Father also predestined that we would become like our elder brother, Jesus: *"For those whom He foreknew—of whom He was aware and loved beforehand—He also destined from the beginning (foreordaining them) to be molded into the image of His Son [and share inwardly His likeness], that He might be the first-born among many brethren."* Note carefully that God has created a new breed of man who will resemble His Son. Jesus is destined to become *"the first born among many brethren."* Wow! What a thought, what a glorious future!

However, although God's power accomplishes the work making us become like His Son, Jesus, we do have a role to play in this process. In 2 Corinthians 3:18 we read: *"But we all, with open face beholding as in a glass the glory of the Lord, are changed into the same image from glory to glory, even as by the Spirit of the Lord."* We must take time to study and absorb God's Word as implied in John 6:51,53,56,57:

> *I am the living bread which came down from heaven: if any man eat of this bread, he shall live for ever: and the bread that I will give is my flesh, which I will give for the life of the world. He that eateth my flesh, and drinketh my blood, dwelleth in me, and I in him. As the living Father hath sent me, and I live by the Father: so he that eateth me, even he shall live by me.*

We need to be aware that the oneness and intimacy that Jesus had with His Father when He walked on earth as a man has been given to human beings. Note that the privilege of 'dwelling in Him and He in us' allows us to reflect His glory.

We Were Born To Greatness and Glory

Our true identity and the fabulous Heavenly assets we possess are revealed to us through the gospel. The gospel is really about how God sent His Son, Jesus, to promote human beings to greatness and glory. However, promotion is contingent on our willingness to put away our rebellion, honor God as our Heavenly Father and Jesus as the Lord of our lives.

The gospel reveals that human beings are sons and daughters of the God of the universe, who is also known as the King of kings and Lord of lords. It is the desire and the will of our Heavenly Father that among the ways His children would resemble Him is by reflecting His glory. Perhaps the most significant revelation of this truth about reflecting God's glory is found in the words of Jesus as He prayed to the Father in the Garden of Gethsemane. This prayer is found in John 17:22: *"And the glory which thou gavest me I have given them; that they may be one, even as we are one."*

In addition to that prayer of Jesus, Isaiah 60:1-3 provide more information concerning our function as reflectors of God's glory: *"Arise, shine; for thy light is come, and the glory of the Lord is risen upon thee. For, behold, the darkness shall cover the earth, and gross darkness the people: but the Lord shall arise upon thee, and his glory shall be seen upon thee. And the Gentiles shall come to thy light, and kings to the brightness of thy rising."*

Note first of all that the glory which we are to reflect originates from God. Secondly, the glory which we must reflect is designed to provide light to a world steeped in darkness (ignorance). And, thirdly, observe that God's glory will be seen on us and will have the effect of drawing many people to Jesus, the true Light.

The writer of Hebrews was so impressed with the glory and honor that God has bestowed on human beings that he penned these words found in Hebrews 2:5-7:

> *And the future world we are talking about will not be controlled by angels. No, for in the book of Psalms David says to God, "What is mere man that you are so concerned about him? And who is this Son of Man You honor so highly? For though You made him lower than the angels for a little while, now You have crowned Him with glory and honor.*

We are Kings and Priests

Revelation 5:10 informs us that among the benefits that Jesus accomplished for us is the provision of a royal heritage: *"And has made us unto our God kings and priests: and we shall reign on the earth."* Information regarding our royal lineage is also found in 1 Peter 2:9: *"But ye are a chosen generation, a royal priesthood, an holy nation, a peculiar people; that ye should shew forth the praises of him who called you out of darkness into his marvelous light."*

Anything We Ask In His Name Will Be Done

Oh what special privileges God has extended to His royal children! Because we are incorporated into Jesus, God considers us as extensions of Himself. Just as branches are parts of the vine and extend from it, in like manner we are parts of Jesus. This is what is meant by using the name of Jesus. In view of the fact that we are not independent entities, but parts of Jesus, we are instructed to use His name and anything we ask will be done. This benefit is expressed by Jesus in John 16:23,24: *"And in that day ye shall ask me nothing. Verily, verily, I say unto you, Whatsoever ye shall ask the Father in my name, he will give it you. Hitherto have ye asked nothing in my name: ask, and ye shall receive, that your joy may be full."* It was the powerful name of Jesus that healed the lame man who sat daily at the temple gate begging. This man was unable to walk and had suffered in this condition from birth. The account is related in Acts 3:4-8:

> *And Peter, fastening his eyes upon him with John, said, Look on us. And he gave heed unto them, expecting to receive something of them. Then Peter said, Silver and gold have I none; but such as I have give I thee: in the name of Jesus Christ of Nazareth rise up and walk. And he took him by the right hand, and lifted him up: and immediately his feet and ancle bones received strength. And he leaping up stood, and walked, and entered with them into the temple, walking, and leaping, and praising God.*

Not Servants but Friends

John 15:5,16 state that not only will we have our petitions answered when we use the name of Jesus, but also our status has been elevated—we are called His friends:

> *Henceforth I call you not servants; for the servant knoweth not what his lord doeth: but I have called you friends; for all things that I have heard of my Father I have made known unto you. Ye have not chosen me, but I have chosen you, and ordained you, that ye should go and bring forth fruit, and that your fruit should remain: that whatsoever ye shall ask of the Father in my name, he may give it you.*

Nothing Shall Be Impossible Unto You

How highly does God esteem human beings? The expressed words of Jesus that nothing shall be impossible to us have always amazed me. Here is a capability we would think belongs to God alone. But God shares this awesome privilege with human beings. Listen to these words of Jesus found in Matthew 17:20 as He responds to His disciples' inquiry concerning their failure to cast out a demonic spirit: *"And Jesus said unto them, because of your unbelief: for verily I say unto you. If ye have faith as a grain of mustard seed, ye shall say unto this mountain, Remove hence to yonder place; and it shall remove; <u>and nothing shall be impossible unto you</u> (Underline supplied)."*

These words reveal that although we are indeed God's over-privileged children, yet most of us are unaware of who we are in Christ. We ought not to be surprised, therefore, that in Romans 8:32 we learn that our Heavenly Father withholds nothing from us: *"He that spared not his own Son, but delivered him up for us all, how shall he not with him also freely give us all things?"*

May God help us to always remember that we are children of the great God of the universe. As children of the Kings of kings and Lord of lords we have both privileges and responsibilities. Let us be committed to arise, shine and reflect God's glory.

CHAPTER 2

Do You Know Who You Are?

To know who we are, we need to be acquainted with our parents. Children are adversely affected when they don't know who their real parents are, because instinctively they understand that branches resemble the tree. In this context we must obtain all the information we can about God for He is indeed our original parent. The Scriptures teach that we were made in the image of God, we exist in Him, we are part of Him and share His eternal life. Moreover, each one of us was made to be a priest and a king. It is essential for us to be aware that God's power within us places on each one of us a heavy responsibility to bless and transform the generation that proceed from our loins, our immediate community and even other nations.

We Were Created To Resemble God

The resemblance we share with God is stated in Genesis 1:26,27:

> *And God said, Let us make man in our image, after our likeness: and let them have dominion over the fish of the sea, and over the fowl of the air, and over every creeping thing that creepeth upon the earth. So God created man in his own image, in the image of God created he him; male and female created he them.*

An important characteristic found in God is holiness. We have been instructed to be holy because God, our parent, is holy. This injunction is declared in 1 Peter 1:14-16: *"As obedient children, not fashioning yourselves according to the former lusts in your ignorance: But as he which hath called you is holy, so be ye holy in all manner of conversation; Because it is written, BE YE HOLY; FOR I AM HOLY."*

Love is another manifested characteristic of God. In spite of all our diverse personalities and idiosyncrasies, one common thread that will be seen in all of God's children is love. In fact, the Scriptures strongly advocate that if we are not manifesting love for others we do not know God. In 1 John 4:7,8 we read, *"Beloved, let us love one another: for love is of God; and every one that loveth is born of God, and knoweth God. He that loveth not knoweth not God. For God is love."*

We Are Parts of God

The members of the Godhead share such oneness that sometimes it is difficult to distinguish one from the other. They cooperate and work together in unity. Remember that Jesus said if we have seen Him we have seen the Father (John 14:9). It is simply amazing that God also included us as parts of Himself. Jesus described us as branches in the Vine (John 15:5); as parts of His body (Ephesians 4:16). Furthermore, in John 14:20 Jesus said, *"At that day ye shall know that I am in my Father, and you in me, and I in you."*

The prayer of Jesus in the Garden of Gethsemane before His crucifixion, provide some more details of the oneness we enjoy with God. In John 17:22,23 Jesus said:

> *And the glory which thou gavest me I have given them; that they may be one, even as we are one; I in them, and thou in me, that they may be made perfect in one; and that the world may know that thou hast sent me, and hast loved them, as thou hast loved me.*

Each One of us is a Priest And a King

Our Heavenly Father is called the King of Kings. It makes sense that all God's children will have royal blood coursing through their veins. Revelation 5:10 declares one of the accomplishments of Jesus: *"And had made us unto our God kings and priests: and we shall reign on the earth."* Despite how we may look or act, no human being is ordinary. In fact, the reason why we behave silly is because we have failed to recognize who we really are. The Scriptures also teach that we have an inheritance, and that we are joint-heirs with Christ. One prayer we should frequently repeat and claim is found in Ephesians 1:17,18:

Dr. Grell Ferdinand

That the God of our Lord Jesus Christ, the Father of glory, may give unto you the spirit of wisdom and revelation in the knowledge of him: The eyes of your understanding being enlightened; that ye may know what is the hope of his calling, and what the riches of the glory of his inheritance in the saints.

Why do we need to pray for our eyes to be enlightened? Because we are unaware of the rich inheritance that awaits us.

Our Words Are Powerful

God does not say things carelessly. He knows that His words have weight and produce results. We, too, ought to be very careful what we say. People who work with dynamite or bombs know how careful they must be. So it is with the tongue. The wise man, Solomon, declares in Proverbs 18:21, *"Death and life are in the power of the tongue: and they that love it shall eat the fruit thereof."* Additionally, in Job 22:28 we read, *"Thou shalt also decree a thing and it shall be established unto thee: and the light shall shine upon thy ways."*

Failure to bless others and even ourselves with our words must be considered lost opportunities. Jesus emphasized this truth with the following words found in Matthew 17:20:

And Jesus said unto them, Because of your unbelief: for verily I say unto you, If ye have faith as a grain of mustard seed, ye shall say unto this mountain, Remove hence to yonder place; and it shall remove; and nothing shall be impossible unto you.

Note, however, that in blessing others we must exercise our faith. According to Jesus, we don't need a lot of faith to remove problems from our lives and the lives of others. God regards our words as so important that Matthew 12:36,37 provide the following admonition: *"But I say unto you, That every idle word that men shall speak, they shall give account thereof in the day of judgment. For by thy words thou shalt be justified, and by thy words thou shalt be condemned."*

Do you remember how Jesus cursed the fig tree, and how it withered up by the next day? What would have happened if Jesus had cursed every tree He saw? What would have happened if Jesus cursed everyone who did not like Him? Did His words have weight? Do your words have weight? In John 20:21 Jesus said, *". . . as my Father hath sent me, even so send I you.* Jesus was the model man. One of the reasons why He came to earth was to show us how human beings ought to speak and act with authority and power. Hebrews 2:11 says, *"For both he that sanctifieth and they who are sanctified are all of one: for which cause he is not ashamed to call them brethren."* The wise man, Solomon endorsed the importance of words. In Proverbs 25:11, Solomon declared: *"A word fitly spoken is like apples of gold in pictures of silver."*

Each One of Us is Like an Earthquake

Never think that you are unimportant and that your influence is negligible. Every one of us is like the epicenter of an earthquake that can shake the surrounding surface of the earth. Romans 14:7 states, *"For none of us liveth to himself, and no man dieth to himself."* Our words and our conduct affect our families, our generations that follow and many others around us. Like a stone thrown into the water, the ripples continue to spread far and wide. Both the righteous and the wicked have influenced the world down through the ages. Deuteronomy 11:6 provides an example of how the entire families of Dathan and Abiram suffered the effects of one wicked act on their part. They had conspired against Moses and God dealt harshly with their rebellion:

> *And what he did unto Dathan and Abiram, the sons of Eliab, the son of Reuben: how the earth opened her mouth, and swallowed them up, and their households, and their tents, and all the substance that was in their possessions, in the midst of all Israel:*

What we do and say affects the welfare of our children and their descendants. In Psalm 37:25,26, the Psalmist declares, *I have been young, and now am old; yet have I not seen the righteous forsaken, nor his seed begging bread. He is ever merciful, and lendeth; and his seed is blessed.*

Here is another powerful promise from God in Isaiah 59:21 that explains how our relationship with God affects our children:

> *As for me, this is my covenant with them, saith the LORD; my spirit that is upon thee, and my words which I have put in thy mouth, shall not*

Dr. Grell Ferdinand

depart out of thy mouth, nor out of the mouth of thy seed, nor out of the mouth of thy seed's seed, saith the LORD, from henceforth and for ever.

We Tend to Devalue Ourselves and Others

Because we are unaware of how much God values all His children, we habitually devalue ourselves and especially other people. Gideon's low self—esteem seems to characterize most of us. In Judges 6:12 we read of his response to the Angel's information that God had chosen him to help save Israel from the Midianites:

> *And the angel of the Lord appeared unto him, and said unto him, The Lord is with thee, thou mighty man of valour. And he said unto him, Oh my Lord, wherewith shall I save Israel? Behold, my family is poor in Manasseh, and I am the least in my father's house. And the Lord said unto him, surely I will be with thee, and thou shalt smite the Midianites as one man.*

Did you notice that although the angel called Gideon a mighty man of valor, he did not see himself as God saw him. God knew that He had designed Gideon to be an outstanding leader and deliverer of the Israelites from the vicious assaults of the Midianites. Gideon insisted that he came from a poor family and he was the most insignificant one among them.

Never, underestimate what God has called you to be and to accomplish. We are royal sons and daughters with unique functions and responsibilities. As the chorus below composed by the author expresses, everybody is special:

Everybody is special
God says everyone is royal
God loves you as much as he loves His Son
May His Spirit fill our hearts with respect for everyone

We need to bear in mind that it is God within us Who accomplishes the work.

God's Power Operates From Within Us

Philippians 2:13 is a powerful revelation of how God operates from within us: *"[Not in your own strength] for it is God Who is all the while effectually at work in you [energizing and creating in you the power and desire], both to will and to work for His good pleasure and satisfaction and delight."*

Matthew 10:1,8 teaches that Jesus has empowered both His early and modern disciples:

> *And when he had called unto him his twelve disciples, he gave them power against unclean spirits, to cast them out, and to heal all manner of sickness and all manner of disease. And as ye go, preach, saying, The kingdom of heaven is at hand. Heal the sick, cleanse the lepers, raise the dead, cast out devils: freely ye have received, freely give.*

This truth that God did not limit His power only to His early disciples is clear as we give heed to these words of Jesus: *"And these signs shall follow <u>them that believe:</u> In my name shall they cast out devils; they shall speak with new tongues; They shall take up serpents; and if they drink any deadly thing, it shall not hurt them; they shall lay hands on the sick, and they shall recover (Mark 16:17,18 underline added)."*

How God Values Each One of Us

How much does God value each one of us? He says to us in Isaiah 13:12 *"I will make a man more precious than fine gold; even a man than the golden wedge of Ophir."*

He follows this declaration about our value with the instruction found in Isaiah 60:1-3:

> *Arise and shine; for thy light is come, and the glory of the LORD is risen upon thee. For, behold, the darkness shall cover the earth, and gross darkness the people: but the LORD shall arise upon thee, and his glory shall be seen upon thee. And the Gentiles shall come to thy light, and kings to the brightness of thy rising.*

Do we understand the glorious plans that God has for us? In Ephesians 1:18 we read: *"The eyes of your understanding being enlightened; that ye may know what is the hope of his calling, and what the riches of the glory of his inheritance in the saints . . .*" Additionally, Ephesians 3:20 declares, *"Now unto him that is able to do exceeding abundantly above all that we ask or think, according to the power that worketh in us . . ."*

In John 17:22,23 we learn that Jesus passed on to us the precious gift of oneness with His Father, the Holy Spirit and Himself: *"And the glory which thou gavest me I have given them; that they may be one, even as we are one: I in them, and thou in me, that they may be made perfect in one; and that the world may know that thou has sent me, and hast loved them, as thou hast loved me."*

Could it be that we are underachievers because we did not know that we are parts of God? May the eyes of our understanding be enlightened. May we begin to recognize that our Heavenly Father expects us as children of His to resemble Him in His love, His care for others and in His accomplishments. Let us arise and shine according to Isaiah 60:1. Let us expect God's power to operate from within us very similar to our elder brother, Jesus. In order to reflect the characteristics of God we must yield ourselves to Him fully.

CHAPTER 3

Your Salvation Is Guaranteed: God Omitted Nothing

Salvation, which includes deliverance from sin and its penalty and joint heir-ship with Jesus, is not a reward that God gives to good people. In reality, salvation is a gift that God has given to every human being in the world. Unfortunately, only a few people believe, agree to accept and receive this Divine gift. It is important to emphasize that God has already done His part in giving the gift to everyone, but human beings do have a role to play: they must believe and receive the gift or suffer the penalty for rejecting God's offer. Many things that are already accomplished in the heavenly realm need to become effective in the earthly realm. Our belief and acceptance of Divine promises provide the catalyst that allows God's word to become effective.

God's Gift is to the Whole World

The truth is that God, in the act of giving His Son, has forgiven everyone and has provided eternal life for everybody in the world. This fact is clearly expressed in John 3:16: *"For God so loved the world, that he gave his only begotten Son, that whosoever believeth in him should not perish, but have everlasting life."* This truth about God's gift to the whole world is also supported in 1 John 4:14 and 5:11: *"And we have seen and do testify that the Father sent the Son to be the Savior of the world. And this is the record, that God hath given to us eternal life, and this life is in his Son."* Notice, the Scripture says that God has given. However, we all know that everyone has not accepted and received it.

God's Removal of the Sin of the World

Is it really true that God's gift of justification (forgiveness) and eternal life has been given to everyone? John the Baptist understood this truth and identified Jesus in John 1:29 as the person who took away the world's sin: *"The next day John seeth Jesus coming unto him, and saith, Behold the Lamb of God, which taketh away the sin of the world."* Moreover, Romans 5:18 supplies some more proof: *"Therefore as by the offence of one judgment came upon all men to condemnation; even so by the righteousness of one the free gift came upon all men unto justification of life."*

John 1:4,9,12 reveal that although the life of Jesus has been given to everyone, not everyone accepts it: *"In him was life; and the life was the light of men. That was the true Light which lighteth every man that cometh into the world. But as many as received him to them gave he power to become the sons of God, even to them that believe on his name:"* In order to give His gift of eternal life to the world God first had to remove the sin of everyone.

The Scriptures teach that God has done His part and indeed has removed sin from the whole world. Moreover, every angle was taken care of, every corner was swept, every base was covered in the Divine removal of sin. However, although the sin of everyone has been taken away, we need to understand that it becomes effective only for those who accept, receive it and repent of their sins. God is disappointed that few believe this essential truth in spite of the fact that He has spoken about His removal of sin again and again. This Scripture found in 2 Corinthians 5:19, 21 provide some interesting details of the process of sin removal by the act of Jesus exchanging places with us: *"To wit, that God was in Christ, reconciling the world unto himself, not imputing their trespasses unto them; and hath committed unto us the word of reconciliation. For he hath made him to be sin for us, who knew no sin; that we might be made the righteousness of God in him."* Notice that there was an exchange. Jesus took our sin and gave us His own righteousness. The thoroughness and completeness of the removal of sin is also shown by the fact that in Hebrews 1:3 the Scriptures teach that Jesus accomplished the task of sin removal and then sat down: *"Who being the brightness of his glory, and the express image of his person, and upholding all things by the word of his power, when he had by himself purged our sins, sat down on the right hand of the Majesty on high;"*

Another way of viewing God's removal of sin from the world is the truth that the eternal death deserved by every human being in the world, because of both inherited and executed sin, was paid when Jesus died. The death penalty that should have been ours because of the breaking of the Law, was satisfied by the death of Jesus. According to Hebrews 2:9 in the eyes of the Father every human being has already died for their sins when Jesus died: *"But we see Jesus, who was made a little lower than the angels for the suffering of death, crowned with glory and honour; that he by the grace of God should taste death for every man."*

Sin has been so thoroughly cleansed that the Bible teaches this amazing truth: when Jesus returns to earth He will not be dealing with sin anymore: *"So also Christ died only once as an offering for the sins of many people; and He will come again, but not to deal again with our sins. This time He will come bringing salvation to all those who are eagerly and patiently waiting for Him* (Hebrews 9:28 NLT).

All Justified and All Raised Up Together With Christ

God has been so generous with His children in this world that at the resurrection of Jesus He positioned the entire human race in His Son. As a result, God gave everyone in the world an opportunity to be saved. Ephesians 2:4,5 (Amplified) declare:

> *But God! So rich is He in His mercy! Because of and in order to satisfy the great and wonderful and intense love with which He loved us, Even when we were dead [slain] by [our own shortcomings and trespasses, He made us alive together in fellowship and in union with Christ. —He gave us the very life of Christ Himself, the same new life with which He quickened Him [for] it is by grace –by His favor and mercy which you did not deserve—that you are saved (delivered from judgment and made partakers of Christ's salvation).*

The Apostle Paul told the heathen people in Athens this amazing truth that everyone is living, moving and existing in Jesus: *"For in him we live, and move, and have our being; as certain also of your own poets have said, for we are also his offspring"* (Acts 17:28). This truth that God provided everyone with an opportunity to be saved is supported by Colossians 1:20 (NLT) which says: *"It was through what His Son did that God cleared a path for everything to come to him—all things in heaven and on earth—for Christ's death on the cross has made peace with God for all by His blood."*

Dr. Grell Ferdinand

When God justifies someone, He declares the person to be guiltless or blameless. In other words the person is considered righteous. Romans 3:23,24 (Amplified) explain that God has justified every human being:

Since all have sinned and are falling short of the honor and the glory which God bestows and receives. [All are justified and made upright and in right standing with God, freely and gratituitously by His grace (His unmerited favor and mercy), through the redemption which is provided] in Christ Jesus.

God fulfilled the promise He had made to bless everyone through Abraham's seed, Jesus. Galatians 3:8 (Amplified) declares: "... *In you shall all the nations of the earth be blessed.*" Moreover, in 1 Corinthians 15:20,21 we read, "*For since by man came death, by man came also the resurrection of the dead. For as in Adam all die, even so in Christ shall all be made alive.*"

God Has Even Removed the Charges Proved Against us

The removal of the charges proved against us takes care of present, past and future sins. Since the role of the law always serves to condemn us, God positioned us in Jesus and removed us from under the condemnation of the law. This powerful truth is revealed in Colossians 2:13-15:

And you, who were dead in trespasses and in the uncircumcision of your flesh— your sensuality, your sinful carnal nature—[God] brought to life together with Christ], having (freely) forgiven us all our transgressions; Having cancelled and blotted out and wiped away the handwriting of the note (or bond) with its legal decrees and demands, which was in force and stood against us—hostile to us. This [note with its regulations, decrees and demands] he set aside and cleared completely out of our way by nailing it to [His] cross.

In addition to the passage above, Galatians 3:23-25 clarifies the relationship between believers and the law:

But before faith came, we were kept under the law, shut up unto the faith which should afterwards be revealed. Wherefore the law was our schoolmaster to bring us unto Christ, that we should be justified by faith. But after that faith is come, we are no longer under a schoolmaster.

If there is any doubt remaining regarding the Christian person's obligations to the ten commandment law, certainly it is cleared once and for all by Galations 5:18 which states, *"But if ye are led of the Spirit, ye are not under the law."*

Is Everybody Saved?

Since the Father has already forgiven the whole world and provided them with the gift of eternal life does this mean that everyone is saved? The answer is no, because although a gift was given it does not necessarily mean that it was accepted, claimed and received. Banks and insurance companies have millions of dollars that rightfully belong to individuals, but remain unclaimed. We need to be aware that only those who believe in Jesus and who claim and receive God's gift of salvation are saved. In fact, because of God's removal of the sin of the world, it is really very foolish for any human being to be lost.

How easy it is to be saved? Romans 10:9,10 declares, *"That if thou shalt confess with thy mouth the Lord Jesus, and shalt believe in thine heart that God hath raised him from the dead, thou shalt be saved."* Therefore, it is easy to be saved. Moreover, the Scripture teaches that God doesn't just save individuals, He delights in saving groups of people who are related to each other. When the keeper of the prison where Paul and Silas were imprisoned, asked the question, *"Sirs, what must I do to be saved?"* He was told, *"Believe on the Lord Jesus Christ, and thou shalt be saved, and thy house"* (Acts 16:30,31). In addition to the passage above, according to 1 Corinthians 7:13,14 unbelieving husbands or wives together with their children are considered holy by God because of the believing spouse:

> *And the woman which hath an husband that believeth not, and if he be pleased to dwell with her, let her not leave him. For the unbelieving husband is sanctified by the wife, and the unbelieving wife is sanctified by the husband: else were your children unclean; but now are they holy.*

This passage of Scripture implies that God saves entire households. Examples of families that were saved are Noah with his family and Abraham with his family. In Isaiah 49:25, God has indicated that He will save our children: *"But thus saith the Lord, Even the captives of the mighty shall be taken away, and the prey of the terrible shall be delivered: for I will contend with him that contendeth with thee, and I will save thy children."*

Dr. Grell Ferdinand

In Isaiah 59:21 God promised to continue His salvation and blessings not only to the immediate household, but also to the grand children:

As for me, this is my covenant with them, saith the Lord; My spirit that is upon thee, and my words which I have put in thy mouth, shall not depart out of thy mouth, nor out of the mouth of thy seed, nor out of the mouth of thy seed's seed, saith the Lord, from henceforth and for ever.

God's Extravagant Help in the Salvation Process

In His Divine wisdom and foreknowledge God had carefully put together all the pieces of our salvation even before the foundation of the world. In fact, God put together such a comprehensive plan that our salvation is guaranteed. God knows our limitations, so after having saved us, He decided that He would not leave us up to ourselves. He gave us His own Holy Spirit to cause us gradually to become like Himself. This extraordinary Divine help is explained in God's new covenant promise in Ezekiel 36:25-27, 29:

Then will I sprinkle clean water upon you, and ye shall be clean: from all your idols, will I cleanse you. A new heart also will I give you, and a new spirit will I put within you: and I will take away the stony heart out of your flesh, and I will give you an heart of flesh. And I will put my spirit within you, and cause you to walk in my statutes, and ye shall keep my judgments, and do them. I will also save you from all your uncleanesses: and I will call for the corn and will increase it, and lay no famine upon you.

God has prophesied (all God's promises are prophecies) that His work upon human beings will be thorough and effective. He omitted nothing. He knew that we would have inherited natural dispositions to sin. Therefore, God provided a solution that would remove the programming we inherited within us that influences us to sin. Giving us a new heart and a new spirit is His method of programming us to become like Him and helping us to perform righteous works.

Someone may be wondering whether God's programming us to perform righteous works takes away our freedom. The response to such a thought is that God performs His programming on those who are willing—the ones He knew would accept Him and become like His Son. We need to be aware that at a glance God sees the end from the beginning. Romans 8:29

(NLT) supports this concept that God knew who would accept Him and set up a thorough plan to save them: *"From the very beginning God decided that those who came to Him—and all along He knew who would—should become like His Son, so that His Son would be the First, with many brothers.* 1 Peter 1:2,4 (NLT) provides further support that at the very beginning of time God knew who would accept Him and He does a thorough work on them so that they would become like His Son, Jesus:

> *Dear friends, God the Father chose you long ago and knew you would become His children. And the Holy Spirit has been at work in your hearts, cleansing you with the blood of Jesus Christ and making you to please Him. May God bless you richly and grant you increasing freedom from all anxiety and fear. And God has reserved for His children the priceless gift of eternal life; it is kept in heaven for you, pure and undefiled, beyond the reach of change and decay. And God in His mighty power, will make sure that you get there safely to receive it, because you are trusting Him. It will be yours in that coming last day for all to see.*

The words and the experience of the Apostle Paul in Galatians 1:15 (Amplified) supports this beautiful truth that God knew long before we were born that we would come to Him, and He sets us apart:

> *But when He Who had chosen and set me apart [even] before I was born, and had called me by His grace (His undeserved favor and blessing, [Isaiah 49:1; Jer.1:5.] Saw fit and was pleased to reveal (unveil, disclose) His Son within me so that I might proclaim Him among the Gentiles [the non-Jewish world] as the glad tidings, immediately I did not confer with flesh and blood—did not consult or counsel with any frail human being or communicate with any one.*

We also need to be aware that after God sets us apart, the change, regeneration or rebirth He initiates and processes in us does not happen overnight. Regeneration goes on gradually over a period of years. Ephesians 4:22-24 (Amplified) implies that regeneration takes time:

> *Strip yourselves of your former nature—put off and discard your old unrenewed self—which characterized your previous manner of life and becomes corrupt through lusts and desires that spring from delusion; And be constantly renewed in the spirit of your mind—having a fresh mental*

and spiritual attitude; And put on the new nature (the regenerate self) created in God's image, (Godlike) in true righteousness and holiness.

We do have a role to play in the process. We must desire to be changed, we must pray for it and cooperate with God. However, we must bear in mind that only God can change us. 2 Corinthians 3:18 states: *"But we all, with open face beholding as in a glass the glory of the Lord, are changed into the same image from glory to glory, even as by the Spirit of the Lord."*

Freed from Sin and Considered Righteous in the Sight of God

God is so generous that while we are still in the process of being changed, He considers us righteous. The fact that we have accepted His gift of salvation and surrendered our lives to Him is sufficient for God to declare that we are righteous. Romans 6:7, 10 state, *"For he that is dead is freed from sin. Likewise reckon ye also yourselves to be dead indeed unto sin, but alive unto God through Jesus Christ our Lord."* The essential role that Jesus plays in the process of our justification is also brought out in the following Scripture:

> *For by the death He died, He died to sin [ending His relation to it] once for all, and the life that He lives He is living to God—in unbroken fellowship with Him. Even so consider yourselves also dead to sin and your relation to it broken, but [that you are] alive to God—living in unbroken fellowship with Him—in Christ Jesus (Romans 6:10 Amplified).*

It is the shared life of Jesus that provides us the privilege of being considered righteous by our Heavenly Father. The fact that those who agree to receive Jesus (to share His life) are indeed considered righteous by God, the Father, is supported by Romans 6:18 (Amplified) *"And having been set free from sin, you have become the servants of righteousness—of conformity to the divine will in thought, purpose and action."* Moreover, Romans 4:5-8 give more details of how this magnanimous God considers us righteous in spite of our weaknesses:

> *But to him that worketh not, but believeth on him that justifieth the ungodly, his faith is counted for righteousness. Even as David also describeth the blessedness of the man, whom God imputeth righteousness without works. Saying, BLESSED ARE THEY WHOSE INIQUITIES*

ARE FORGIVEN, AND WHOSE SINS ARE COVERED. BLESSED IS THE MAN TO WHOM THE LORD WILL NOT IMPUTE SIN.

If everyone in the world understood the generosity of God and the extent to which all human beings have been loved, forgiven and promoted, it is likely that more people will accept God's awesome gifts. Let us believe that our Heavenly Father has done everything to save us.

CHAPTER 4

The Lord Jesus is Man's Substitute

Our Heavenly Father positioned all human beings in His Son Jesus at the cross. We all died when Jesus died, and we were all resurrected in Jesus when He was resurrected. However, this gift God gave us to operate in oneness with the Godhead only becomes effective when we believe it. Because God positioned us in Christ, we share His life, His name, His identity, His victory and His anointing. This unification of God and man displays our Father's profound wisdom, His intense love for us and the value He places on all mankind. In this act we see a Divine tactical strategy that hid our lives in Jesus who represents us totally.

1 John 4:9 summarizes the substitutional role of Jesus and what was accomplished at the cross: "*In this was manifested the love of God toward us, because that God sent his only begotten Son into the world, that we might live through him.*"

Man's Integration with Christ

We need to remember that God does many things in advance. 2 Timothy 1:9 declares some of the things God did long before we became aware of His actions: "*Who saved us, and called us with an holy calling, not according to our works, but according to his own purpose and grace, which was given us in Christ Jesus before the world began.*"

God acted first (saved us first) and our belief comes after the fact. His intense love for all His children caused Him to act on our behalf even without our consent. Of course, we must emphasize that our belief and our acceptance allow Divine benefits to become effective. God has also raised us up together with Christ at His resurrection without our consent. This fact is expressed in Ephesians 2:6 (Amplified): "*And He raised us up together with Him and made us sit down together—giving us joint seating with him—in the heavenly sphere [by virtue of our being] in Christ Jesus, the*

Messiah, the Annointed One." In a brief summary of the above passages of Scripture, we learn that:

(1) God works on our behalf before we become aware of His kind acts.
(2) He shared with us the very life of Christ and His anointing.
(3) Our joint seating with Christ means we are joint-heirs with Him.
(4) We did not initiate this act. It was purely God's doing.

We are Branches in the Vine

The words of Jesus in John 15:5,6 support the truth that we are strategically positioned in Him. Like branches in a vine, we are all extensions of Jesus and we are to abide and depend on Him totally. Note that abiding in Him is a conscious choice that we must make:

> *Abide in me, and I in you. As the branch cannot bear fruit of itself, except it abide in the vine; no more can ye, except ye abide in me. I am the vine, ye are the branches: He that abideth in me, and I in him, the same bringeth forth much fruit: for without me ye can do nothing. If a man abide not in me, he is cast forth as a branch, and is withered; and men gather them, and cast them into the fire, and they are burned.*

God's Representative System

It is essential for us to understand that God has established a representative system in which one person acts as a representative or agent for a group of other individuals. This truth is clearly revealed in the Biblical account of David's defeat of Goliath. In this account, David represented his people, the kingdom of Israel, while Goliath represented the Philistines. In 1 Samuel 17: 8,9 God used Goliath to express this very important concept of one person representing his entire group:

> *And he stood and cried unto the armies of Israel, and said unto them, Why are ye come out to set your battle in array? am not I a Philistine, and ye servants to Saul? Choose you a man for you, and let him come down to me. If he be able to fight with me, and to kill me, then will we be your servants: but if I prevail against him, and kill him, then shall ye be our servants, and serve us.*

Observe that that the fate of each group rested on the performance of one man. David prevailed, killed Goliath and won the battle for Israel. David portrayed the role of our Savior, Jesus, who won the battle for the entire human race against the forces of darkness. David understood that it was the Lord who fought the battle, and spoke these significant words found in 1 Samuel 17:47: *"This day will the Lord deliver thee into mine hand . . . And all this assembly shall know that the Lord saveth not with sword and spear: for the battle is the Lord's, and he will give you into our hands."*

The Comprehensive Function of Jesus as Man's Substitute

In John 14:6 Jesus revealed the extensive range of benefits He brings to us in His role as man's substitute: *"I am the way, the truth, and the life: no man cometh unto the Father, but by me."* The Son of God's all-embracing substitutional work for everyone is also reflected in His declaration found in John 11:25,26: *"Jesus said unto her, I am the resurrection, and the life: he that believeth in me, though he were dead, yet shall he live: and whosoever liveth and believeth in me shall never die. Believest thou this?"*

Our Substitute, Jesus, Supplies all our Needs

It should be emphasized that as man's substitute, not only has Jesus suffered the death that should have been ours, but He shares His life with us. Because we live in Him, He is responsible for supplying all of our needs every moment of every day. This truth is expressed in Philippians 4:19: *"But my God shall supply all your need according to his riches in glory by Christ Jesus."*

Our Substitute Supplies our Obedience

One of the essential benefits human beings enjoy because of Jesus' role as our substitute is the transfer of His obedience to us. As a result, Jesus satisfies all the demands of the Law for us. This truth is expressed in Romans 5:18,19: *"Therefore as by the offense of one judgment came upon all men to condemnation; even so by the righteousness of one the free gift came upon all men unto justification of life. For as by one man's disobedience many were made sinners, so by the obedience of one shall many be made righteous."*

The Scripture above also supports the fact that God has a representative system. Notice that one man (Adam's sin) had brought condemnation to the entire human race. The second Adam, Jesus, did the opposite by bringing us forgiveness and His obedience. Our acceptance of Jesus as our substitute delivers us from the condemnation of the law. Romans 8:1-3 explain it:

> There is therefore now no condemnation to them which are in Christ Jesus, who walk not after the flesh, but after the Spirit. For the law of the Spirit of life in Christ Jesus hath made me free from the law of sin and death. For what the law could not do in that it was weak through the flesh, God sending his own Son in the likeness of sinful flesh, and for sin condemned sin in the flesh:

Jesus is Our Righteousness

As man's substitute, Jesus is our righteousness. This glorious truth is found in Jeremiah 23:6: *"In his days Judah shall be saved, and Israel shall dwell safely: and this is his name whereby he shall be called, THE LORD OUR RIGHTEOUSNESS."*

Moreover, Isaiah 61:10 explains that there is great need for believers to rejoice because we are clothed in the righteousness of Jesus: *"I will greatly rejoice in the Lord, my soul shall be joyful in my God; for he hath clothed me with the garments of righteousness, as a bridegroom decketh himself with ornaments, and as a bride adorneth herself with her jewels."*

Jesus Supplies our Wisdom

Our Heavenly Father has designed it so that Jesus, our substitute, will also supply our wisdom if we allow Him. 1 Corinthians 1:30 declares: *"But of him are ye in Christ Jesus, who of God is made unto us wisdom, and righteousness, and sanctification, and redemption:"* We are very fortunate to have been positioned in Jesus for Colossians 2:3 (Amplified) states concerning the wealth of knowledge and wisdom stored in Him: *"In Him all the treasures of [divine] wisdom, [of comprehensive insight into the ways and purposes of God], and [all the riches of spiritual knowledge and enlightenment are stored up and lie hidden."*

The Victory of Jesus is Ours

As our substitute, Jesus even provides us with His victory over sin, death and the devil. This truth is expressed in 1 Corinthians 15:56,57: *"The sting of death is sin; and the strength of sin is the law. But thanks be to God which giveth us the victory through our Lord Jesus Christ."* Because His victory is ours, we are admonished in Psalms 98:1 to be joyful and to sing His praises: *"O sing unto the Lord a new song; for he hath done marvelous things: his right hand, and his holy arm hath gotten him the victory."*

Blameless in God's Sight

Since every person who accepts the substitute function of Jesus receives His wisdom, obedience, righteousness, sanctification and redemption, our acceptance of these gifts causes us to be considered blameless in the sight of our Heavenly Father. This fantastic benefit is expressed in Ephesians 1:4,11 (LNT):

> *Long ago, even before He made the world, God chose us to be His very own, through what Christ would do for us: He decided then to make us holy in His eyes, without a single fault—we who stand before Him covered with His love. Moreover, because of what Christ has done we have become gifts to God that He delights in, for as part of God's sovereign plan we were chosen from the beginning to be His, and all things happen just as He decided long ago.*

It is important for us to understand that our acceptance by our Heavenly Father is not a temporary status. For how long will believers enjoy God's acceptance and the privileged state of blamelessness in His sight? 1 Corinthians 1:8 (Amplified) explains: *"And He will establish you to the end—keep you steadfast, give you strength, and guarantee your vindication, that is, be your warrant against all accusation or indictment—[so that you will be] guiltless and irreproachable in the day of our Lord Jesus Christ, the Messiah."*

Another exciting privilege and also a demonstration of the effectiveness of the work of Jesus as our substitute is the indwelling of God's Holy Spirit. Obviously, the Holy Spirit could not live in an unholy environment. The Scriptures state that each one of us is the temple of the Holy Ghost, and of course, God cannot lie. In 1 Corinthians 3:16,17 we read: *"Know ye not that ye are the temple of God, and that the Spirit of God dwelleth in you? If any man defile the temple of God, him shall God destroy; for the temple of God is holy, which temple ye are.*" To be the temple of the Holy Ghost we must be holy in God's eyes. Isn't this a marvelous reality?

All of these passages of Scripture declare how fortunate human beings are and how generous God is! Colossians 2:9-15 (LNT) provide a summary of God's generosity toward mankind in sending Jesus to be our substitute:

> *For in Christ there is all of God in a human body; So you have everything when you have Christ, and you are filled with God through your union with Christ. He is the highest ruler, with authority over every other power. You were dead in sins, and your sinful desires were not yet cut away. Then he gave you a share in the very life of Christ, for he forgave all your sins, and blotted out the charges proved against you, the list of commandments which you had not obeyed. He took this list of sins and destroyed it by nailing it to Christ's cross. In this way God took away Satan's power to accuse you of sin, and God openly displayed to the whole world Christ's triumph at the cross where your sins were all taken away.*

In the Very Presence of God

Another glorious benefit of the substitution effected by Jesus is the fact that we are now positioned in the very presence of God. Therefore, not only are we considered blameless in His sight, but we are to enjoy His presence. This truth is revealed in Colossians 1:20-22:

> *You were His enemies and hated him and were separated from Him by your evil thoughts and actions, yet now He has brought you back as His friends. He has done this through the death on the cross of His own human body, <u>and now as a result Christ has brought you into the very presence of God, and you are standing there before Him with nothing left against you—nothing that He could even chide you for:</u>" (Underline supplied).*

The Lord Jesus Is Our New Identity

It is essential that we begin to picture ourselves as small parts of a whole. We are totally enveloped by Christ and hidden in Him. That is where the Father placed us, and that is how He sees us. Colossians 3:3 states, "*For ye are dead, and your life is hid with Christ in God. When Christ, who is our life, shall appear, then shall ye also appear with him in glory."*

This reality that we are hidden in Christ is supported in Galatians 3:27 (LNT): *"And we who have been baptized into union with Christ are enveloped by Him."* Because we are in the Lord He has become our strength and our shield. In Isaiah 12:2 we read, *"Behold, God is my salvation; I will trust, and not be afraid: for the Lord JE-HO-VAH is my strength and my song; he is become my salvation."* Notice that the author did not merely say that God gave him salvation, but that the Lord is his salvation. This thought is repeated in Psalm 27:1 where David exclaims, *"The Lord is my light and my salvation: whom shall I fear? The Lord is the strength of my life; of whom shall I be afraid?"*

We must stop thinking that each one of us is a separate entity from Jesus. When Saul (whose name was changed to Paul) persecuted the early believers, the Lord called out to him one day when he was traveling on the road to Damascus in his hunt for more Christians to persecute. Note how the Lord identified Himself with believers according to Acts 9:3-5 (LNT):

> *As he was nearing Damascus on this mission, suddenly a brilliant light from heaven spotted down upon him! He fell to the ground and heard a voice saying to him, "Saul! Saul! Why are you persecuting Me?" "Who is speaking, sir?" Paul asked. And the voice replied, "I am Jesus, the one you are persecuting!"*

God's representative system has defeated the cunning Satanic plots against all human beings whose lives are hidden in Jesus. This fusion of God and man brought salvation to everyone who believes and accepts Jesus as their substitute and their salvation. May God open our eyes to understand and appreciate the glorious truth of who we really are in Christ. May the power of the Holy Spirit and the love of God be manifested in our daily lives as God displays His Son in us.

CHAPTER 5

Fight the Good Fight of Faith Lay Hold on Eternal Life

Imagine that you are in a deep well, and because you are unable to get out you are obviously facing death. Someone throws you a rope and instructs you to lay hold of the rope so you could be pulled to safety. Be aware that you have been given the choice of either exercising faith in the rescuer by grasping the rope that leads to safety, or refusing help and perishing. Faith is the rope and Jesus is the One who rescues us from problems we face in this world, from the pit of hell and eternal death. How important is the exercise of our faith? Our eternal life, our righteousness, our healing, the satisfaction of our need for urgent miracles—all these are dependent on our faith.

1 Timothy 6:12, declares, *"Fight the good fight of faith, lay hold on eternal life, whereunto thou art also called, and hast professed a good profession before many witnesses."* From this Scripture we learn first of all that faith entails a fight and therefore, demands bravery, courage and skill. Moreover, our safety, success and eternal future is dependent on our faith. Since the exercise of faith is so crucial to our survival and success, we need to study what faith is, how it operates and how to obtain it.

Faith Defined

One of the clearest and most challenging explanations of what faith consists of is given in Hebrews 11:1 (NLT): *"Faith is the confidence that what we hope for will actually happen; it gives us assurance about things we cannot see."* Webster's dictionary defines confidence as "Trust in or reliance upon something or someone; belief in a person or thing." Faith in God involves trusting Him and believing we have things that we do not see. Most of us who are Christians assert that we have faith in God. However, here are some challenging questions we need to ask ourselves: (a) Are we confidently expecting that which we request from God to actually happen? Or is there an "if" or "maybe" involved? (b) How long are we prepared to wait confidently for our expectations? Our responses to these questions reflect our level of faith.

Waiting—An Important Component of Faith

The Scriptures state a whole lot about waiting on God, because faith involves waiting confidently. Psalm 27:14 declares, *"Wait on the Lord: be of good courage, and he shall strengthen thine heart: wait, I say, on the LORD."* Again, in Isaiah 40:31 we are given some benefits that are received from waiting on God: *"But they that wait upon the LORD shall renew their strength; they shall mount up with wings as eagles; they shall run, and not be weary; and they shall walk, and not faint."*

Abraham, who became famous for his tremendous faith in God, was seventy-five years old when God told him he would have a son. He kept on waiting on God and Isaac, the promised son was born when Abraham was one hundred years old. David, another man of faith, was anointed king of Israel when he was just a youth. He actually became king several years later when Saul died. Waiting on God's time is such a critical component of faith that God always gives special rewards to those who wait on Him. In fact, some of the outstanding persons who waited on God in the past are listed in His Hall of Fame in Hebrews Chapter eleven. On the other hand, those who refuse to wait on God experience His displeasure.

The Bible records that on several occasions the children of Israel refused to wait on God. Whenever there was scarcity of some kind, they complained and criticized Moses, God's chosen leader. Psalm 106:13,21-23 describe their wrong attitude and how God reacted:

They soon forgat his works; they waited not for his counsel: They forgat God their saviour, which had done great things in Egypt; Wondrous works in the land of Ham, and terrible things by the Red sea. Therefore he said that he would destroy them, had not Moses his chosen stood before him in the breach, to turn away his wrath, lest he should destroy them.

The Israelites praised and believed God only for short periods of time when they saw the miracles that satisfied their needs. God wants His people to trust Him and believe His word even when there is nothing to see.

By Faith and Not by Sight

The principle of walking by faith and not by sight is mentioned in 2 Corinthians 5:7 (NI): "*We live by faith, not by sight.*" 2 Kings chapters six and seven recount the punishment an Israelite officer received because he operated by sight and not by faith. The Israelites in Samaria were besieged by King Benhadad of Aram. As a result the Israelites who lived in Samaria experienced such a severe famine that two women made an agreement to kill their two children and share their cooked bodies with each other.

When Elisha announced that the famine would come to an end, an officer who assisted the King of Israel, expressed his skepticism that such a thing could happen. 2 Kings 7:1,2 (NLT) recall how the Lord punished the officer for his lack of faith:

> *Elisha replied, "Listen to this message from the LORD! This is what the LORD says: By this time tomorrow in the markets of Samaria, five quarts of choice flour will cost only one piece of silver, and ten quarts of barley grain will cost only one piece of silver." The officer assisting the king said to the man of God, "That couldn't happen even if the LORD opened the windows of heaven!" But Elisha replied, "You will see it happen with your eyes, but you won't be able to eat any of it!"*

Subsequently, the Lord caused the invaders to hear sounds like a large enemy army was about to attack them. They immediately ran away leaving their food, silver, gold, clothing and other valuables behind. Some Israelite lepers who ventured into the enemy camp in search of food discovered that the invaders were no longer there. They collected some valuables, hid some for themselves and announced to the other people of Israel that the danger had subsided. The Israelites rushed out and took all the resources which the invading army had left in their haste to escape.

Meanwhile, the King of Israel had ordered his officer to control the people who were rushing in and out the gate of the city. The officer who had positioned himself at the gate, was knocked down and trampled by the hordes of people. This officer was punished severely because he walked by sight and not by faith.

Dr. Grell Ferdinand

Make Your Request and Believe that You Have It

To practice walking by faith and not by sight, we must believe that we have the requested result before it actually happens. Moreover, we must be prepared to begin thanking God for results before we see them. Jesus spoke about this principle in Mark 11:24: *"Therefore I say unto you, What things soever ye desire, when ye pray, believe that ye receive them, and ye shall have them."* Our first instruction mentioned in this Scripture is to believe that we have what we asked for. This verb is in the present tense. The second verb states that we shall receive them. This verb is in the future tense. The principle being taught signifies that there may be a short or long period of waiting confidently before we actually see results. God has been known to give tremendous rewards to those who patiently, confidently wait on Him.

Eternal Life—A Reward for Exercising Faith

We ought to learn from Israel's experiences that God is very displeased with our lack of faith. On the other hand, God rewards our faith with amazing gifts including eternal life. Jesus provides good news about the connection between eternal life and faith in John 5:24 (NLT): *"I tell you the truth, those who listen to my message and believe in God who sent me have eternal life. They will never be condemned for their sins, but they have already passed from death unto life."* Can we speak with certainty that we have eternal life? Here is another Scripture that confirms that we do have eternal life. It's found in 1 John 5:11,13 (NLT):

> And this is what God has testified: He has given us eternal life, and this life is in his Son. Whosoever has the Son has life; whosoever does not have God's Son does not have life. I have written this to you who believe in the name of the Son of God, so that you may know you have eternal life.

Note that there is no if, but or maybe in this Scripture. Moreover, note that eternal life is not simply a gift we will receive in the future. We are encouraged to know with certainty that believers have eternal life at the present time.

Righteousness—Another Reward for Exercising Faith

When someone exercises faith in God and His Son, Jesus, the righteousness of Jesus is immediately imputed to the person. A righteous person is considered by God to be without sin. Here are some reassuring words given to us in Romans 3:21-24 (NLT):

> *But now God has shown us a way to be made right with him without keeping the requirements of the law, as was promised in the writing of Moses and the prophets long ago. We are made right with God by placing our faith in Jesus Christ. And this is true for everyone who believes, no matter who we are. For everyone has sinned; we all fall short of God's glorious standard. Yet God with undeserved kindness, declared that we are righteous.*

Oh, what marvelous love and kindness this is for God to declare us acceptable and righteous in His sight because we exercise faith in Him!

In addition to the above, here is what Romans 4:2,3 state about the rewards of righteousness that Abraham received for exercising faith in God: *"For if Abraham were justified by works, he hath whereof to glory; but not before God. For what saith the scripture? ABRAHAM BELIEVED GOD, AND IT WAS COUNTED UNTO HIM FOR RIGHTEOUSNESS."* We can take heart when we examine ourselves and find all kinds of faults which obviously can bring us discouragement. God considers us righteous because of our faith in Him.

Healing—A Reward for the Exercise of Faith

There are several instances in the Bible where faith exercised by human beings caused them to be healed. Matthew 9:27-30 (NLT) recalls the healing of two blind men who demonstrated faith in God. This miracle was done soon after Jesus had resurrected the dead daughter of the leader of the synagogue:

> *After Jesus left the girl's home, two blind men followed along behind him, shouting, "Son of David, have mercy upon us!" They went right into the home where he was staying, and Jesus asked them, "Do you believe I can make you see?" "Yes, Lord," they told him, "we do." Then he touched their*

eyes and said, "Because of your faith, it will happen." Then their eyes were opened, and they could see! . . .

In another incident Jesus healed a woman who had an issue of blood for twelve years. The Scripture recounted that she had spent all her money on physicians but had remained sick. She came and touched the border of Jesus' garment and was immediately healed. Luke 8:47,48 describes the encouraging words spoken to her by Jesus: *"And he said unto her, Daughter, be of good comfort: thy faith hath made thee whole; go in peace."*

The Origin of Faith

Let there be no misunderstanding: any faith found in human beings comes from God. From what we have studied so far, we ought to be convinced that faith is indeed a good gift. James 1:17 informs us that God is the source of every good gift: *"Every good gift and every perfect gift is from above, and cometh down from the Father of lights, with whom is no variableness, neither shadow of turning."* Hebrews 10:17 states, *"So then faith cometh by hearing, and hearing by the word of God."* This Scripture encourages us to build up our faith by constantly reading the Word, meditating on it and listening to others preach and teach. In Acts 3:46 we learn that the early church met every day studying the Word: *"And they, continuing daily with one accord in the temple, and breaking bread from house to house, did eat their meat with gladness and singleness of heart . . ."*

Some Outstanding Accomplishments of Faith

Hebrews 11:33,34 provide us with some fascinating results of what faith accomplished in Bible times. These accounts should inspire us to build and exercise our faith to obtain similar results:

Who through faith subdued kingdoms, wrought righteousness, obtained promises, stopped the mouth of lions, Quenched the violence of fire, escaped the edge of the sword, out of weakness were made strong, waxed valiant in fight, turned to flight the armies of aliens. Women received their dead raised to life again: and others were tortured, not accepting deliverance; that they might obtain a better resurrection.

Why should we be building our faith every day? From what we have studied, faith helps us to obtain eternal life (salvation), righteousness, healing and the fulfillment of urgent needed miracles. In addition, we are admonished in Hebrews 11:6: *"But without faith it is impossible to please him: for he that cometh to God must believe that he is, and that he is a rewarder of them that diligently seek him."*

CHAPTER 6

It Is God

Philippians 2:13 declares, *"For it is God which worketh in you both to will and to do of his good pleasure."* This Scripture plainly states that God is the One Who does all the work, while His followers are merely instruments in His hands through whom He operates. Not only does God do the work Himself, it is He who causes His followers to become willing to obey Him. The Holy Spirit was not given to us to become an idle, observant passenger, but to be the driver and the engine. Unfortunately, the tendency to exaggerate our functions sets limits on God's effectiveness for us and through us. Even outstanding Biblical leaders including Moses and Elijah had failed at some stage in their lives to understand the principle of total dependence on God. Whether our needs are for salvation, protection, physical necessities and even prayers, it is God Who must be invited and allowed to do it all.

It Is Not You But God Who Began It And It Is God Who Will Complete It

In the salvation process we can never exaggerate the human function when we truly understand that it is God Who chose us to be His followers, and it is God Who will complete the work in and for us. John 15:16 (NI) is very clear regarding who does all the work: *"You did not choose me, but I chose you and appointed you to go and bear fruit—fruit that will last. Then the Father will give you whatever you ask in my name."* As Christians, some of us may think that we should be commended for choosing Christ as Lord of our lives. No, No, No! It is God Who chose us. Note how the following Scripture in Philippians 1:6 (NAS) dovetails into the previous one: *"For I am confident of this very thing, that he who began a good work in you will perfect it until the day of Christ Jesus."* Who began it? God did. Who will continue and complete it? God will.

The Father Spoke And Worked Through Jesus

As our human example, Jesus taught and demonstrated the principle of depending on God to do everything for Him. In John 5:30 Jesus declared:

I am able to do nothing from Myself [independently, of My own accord—but only as I am taught by God and as I get his orders]. Even as I hear, I judge [I decide as I am bidden to decide. As the voice comes to Me, so I give a decision], and My judgment is right (just, righteous) because I do not seek or consult My own will [I have no desire to do what is pleasing to Myself, My own aim, My own purpose] but only the will and pleasure of the Father Who sent Me.

Obviously, this truth of total dependence on God contradicts the erroneous concept (held by many) that God helps those who help themselves.

In John 14:10-12 the importance of allowing God to work through us is again taught by Jesus in the following words:

Believest not that I am in the Father, and the Father in me? The words that I speak unto you I speak not of myself: but the Father that dwelleth in me, he doeth The works. Believe me that I am in the Father, and the Father in me: or else believe me for the very works sake. Verily, verily, I say unto you, He that believeth in me, the works that I do shall he do also; and greater works than these shall he do; because I go unto my Father.

In order for us to do similar works like Jesus or greater works, we must follow His modus operandi or His methods of submitting our will to God and allowing Him to speak and work through us. Let us always remember that we were not created to live on our own, but to depend wholly on God.

Why Human Beings Cannot Successfully Do It Alone

The expression 'God helps those who help themselves' implies that there are times when we ought to be acting independently of God. However, human beings were never created to operate independently, for we were created in the image of God (Genesis 1:27). Even the members of the Godhead, the Father, the Holy Spirit and Jesus are interdependent. They always act in concert and that is why they are referred to as One God. The fact that human beings were created to share in that oneness is expressed by Jesus in His prayer in John 17:20-23:

> *Neither pray I for these alone, but for them also which shall believe on me through their word; That they all may be one; as thou, Father art in me, and I in thee, that they also may be believe that thou hast sent me. And the glory which thou gavest me I have given them; that they may be one, even as we are one. I in them, and thou in me, that they may be perfect in one; and that the world may know that thou hast sent me, and hast loved them, as thou hast loved me.*

In addition, concerning how human beings were created to operate, Jesus said in John 15:5: *"I am the vine, ye are the branches: He that abideth in me, and I in him, the same bringeth forth much fruit: for without me ye can do nothing."* Branches are totally dependent on the tree or vine, constantly receiving and conveying leaves, flowers and or fruits. In addition, the Scriptures refer to human beings in 1 Corinthians 12:4-6,12, not as independent entities but as parts of the body of Christ:

> *Now there are diversities of gifts, but the same Spirit. And there are differences of administrations, but the same Lord. And there are diversities of operations, but it is the same God which worketh all in all. For as the body is one, and hath many members, and all the members of that one body, being many, are one body: so also is Christ.*

It Is God Who Saved Us

In the salvation process, it is God Who does everything from start to finish, while our role is to believe, receive and exhibit what we receive. This truth about God's pervasive involvement in our salvation is expressed in 2 Timothy 1:9: *"Who hath saved us, and called us with an holy calling, not according to our works, but according to his own purpose and grace, which was given us in Christ Jesus before the world began."* Did you notice that salvation was given to us as a gift before we were even born? Jesus took the death we deserved from the foundation of the world (Revelation 13:8). His death is also mentioned in Hebrews 2:9: *"But we see Jesus, who was made a little lower than the angels for the suffering of death, crowned with glory and honor; that he by the grace of God should taste death for every man."*

However, it is true that we can reject the gift of salvation. This truth regarding human choice is expressed in John 1:11-13:

He came unto his own, and his own received him not. But as many as received him, to them gave he power to become the sons of God, even to them that believe on his name: which were born, not of blood, nor of the will of the flesh, nor of the will of man, but of God.

It is interesting that Ephesians 2:4-7 (NLT) declare that we were spiritually dead when God saved us:

But God is so rich in mercy, and he loved us so much, that even though we were dead because of our sins, he gave us life when he raised Christ from the dead. (it is only by God's grace that you have been saved!) For he raised us from the dead along with Christ and seated us with him in the heavenly realms because we are united with Christ Jesus.

The truth that it is God Who continues to sustain us after He saved us is brought out in 1 Corinthians 1:8 (Amplified): *"And He will establish you to the end—keep you steadfast, give you strength, and guarantee your vindication, that is, be your warrant against all accusation or indictment—[so that you will be] guiltless and irreproachable in the day of our Lord Jesus Christ, the Messiah."*

Moses Did Not Understand That It Is God . . .

In the dialogue between God and Moses recorded in Exodus chapters three and four, God was trying to explain to Moses that He was about to free the Israelites from Egyptian slavery. Moses was given a secondary role as a mouthpiece for God. He would be an instrument in God's hands. However, Moses kept talking about his own human limitations, for he thought God was asking him to do an impossible task. Moses did not understand that it is God Who works through human beings. Exodus 3:7,8 (NLT) record the part of the dialogue where God introduces His freedom plan to Moses:

Then the LORD told him, "I have certainly seen the oppression of my people in Egypt. I have heard their cries of distress because of their harsh slave drivers. Yes, I am aware of their suffering. So I have come down to rescue them from the power of the Egyptians and lead them out of Egypt into their own fertile and spacious land. It is a land flowing with milk and honey-the land where the Canaanites, Hittites, Aamorites, Perizzites, Hivites, and Jebusites now live.

Please observe that God made it clear that He came down to accomplish the task.

The secondary role Moses would play is recorded in Exodus 3:9 (NLT): *"Now go, for I am sending you to Pharaoh. You must lead my people, Israel out of Egypt."* At the time when God first introduced His plans, Moses did not understand that his was a secondary role, and that God retained the primary role. So, in Exodus 3:11, Moses, with an exaggerated perception of his responsibilities, argued with God: *"But Moses protested to God, "Who am I to appear before Pharaoh? Who am I to lead the people of Israel out of Egypt?"* In Exodus 3:15 God explained that He was the same God that took care of the needs of the forefathers: *"And God said moreover unto Moses, thus shalt thou say unto the children of Israel, The LORD GOD of your fathers, the God of Abraham, the God of Isaac, and the God of Jacob, hath sent me unto you: this is my name for ever, and this is my memorial unto all generations."*

Even after God performed two miracles, changing Moses' rod into a serpent, and causing his hand to temporarily become leprous, Moses still did not understand God's role. The following dialogue between God and Moses in Exodus 4:10-12 shows that Moses did not understand that it is God Who works through us:

> *And Moses said unto the LORD, O my Lord, I am not eloquent, neither hereto fore, nor since thou hast spoken unto thy servant: but I am slow of speech, and of a slow tongue. And the LORD said unto him, Who hath made man's mouth or who maketh the dumb, or deaf, or the seeing, or the blind? Have not I the LORD? Now therefore go, and I will be with thy mouth, and teach thee what thou shalt say.*

God patiently made an arrangement for Aaron, the brother of Moses to become the mouthpiece of Moses and explained the details in Exodus 4:15,16:

> *And thou shalt speak unto him, and put words in his mouth: and I will be with thy mouth, and with his mouth, and will teach you what ye shall do.*

And he shall be thy spokesman unto the people: and he shall be, even he shall
be to thee instead of a mouth, and thou shalt be to him instead of God.

In this detailed explanation of how the operation was to be executed, God is giving us insights about His plan to speak and operate through those human beings who submit their lives to Him.

What Elijah Forgot

After Elijah had crested the mountain top of robust faith and demonstrated God's power working through him at Mount Carmel, he suddenly forgot that it is God who protects us. According to the account in 1 Kings 19:1, Jezebel was informed that the prophets of Baal had been slain. She grew very annoyed with Elijah and promised to take His life according to 1 Kings 19:2,3:

Then Jezebel sent a messenger unto Elijah, saying, So let the gods do to me,
and more also, if I make not thy life as the life of one of them by tomorrow
about this time. And when he saw that, he arose, and went for his life, and
came to Beersheba, which belongeth to Judah, and left his servant there.

Apparently, Elijah had hoped that the tremendous miracle God had accomplished through him would have convinced everyone including Jezebel to reject idol worship and recognize Jehovah as their God. His disappointment made him lose sight of the fact that it was primarily God Who was rejected by Jezebel.

It Is God Who Protects Us

Let us always remember that God considers us to be not merely His children, bur also parts of Himself. Would God protect the apple of His eye? In Zechariah 2:8 God calls us the apple of His eye: *"For thus saith the Lord of hosts, After the glory hath he sent me unto the nations which spoiled you: for he that toucheth you toucheth the apple of his eye."* Psalm 46:1-5 capture the responsibility God has taken on Himself to protect us from all evil and free us from our fears:

God is our refuge and strength, a very present help in trouble. Therefore will not we fear, though the earth be removed, and though the mountains be carried into the midst of the sea; Though the waters thereof roar and be troubled, though the mountains shake with the swelling thereof. There is a river, the streams whereof shall make glad the city of God, the holy place of the tabernacles of the most High. God is in the midst of her; she shall not be moved: God shall help her, and that right early.

Wow! Even though the earth moves away from its axis, we are instructed to be fearless because we are protected by an Omnipotent God. Here is another promise of protection found in Isaiah 43:1,2:

But now thus saith the LORD that created thee, O Jacob, and he that formed thee, O Israel, Fear not: for I have redeemed thee, I have called thee by thy name; thou art mine. When thou passest through the waters, I will be with thee; and through the rivers, they shall not overflow thee: when thou walkest through the fire, thou shalt not be burned; neither shall the flame kindle upon thee.

We also need to remember that when enemies attack us they are in fact attacking God because we are positioned in Him. We recall that according to Acts 9:3-5 Saul, who later was called the Apostle Paul, had been persecuting the Christians of the early church. Jesus told him that it was He that Saul had been persecuting:

As he was approaching Damascus on this mission, a light from heaven suddenly shone down around him. He fell to the ground and heard a voice saying to him, "Saul! Saul! Why are you persecuting me?" "Who are you, lord?" Saul asked. And the voice replied, "I am Jesus, the one you are persecuting! Now get up and go into the city, and you will be told what you must do."

Isn't it interesting that Saul thought that he was doing God a service by stamping out heresy? He was actually persecuting Jesus because Christians are considered by God to be parts of His Son, Jesus.

God has also taken on the responsibility of fighting our enemies. Isaiah 54:17 states: *"No weapon that is formed against thee shall prosper; and every tongue that shall rise against thee in judgment thou shalt condemn. This is the heritage of the servants of the LORD, and their righteousness is of me, saith the Lord."*

It Is God Who Satisfies All Our Needs

The nature of Divine involvement in supplying all our needs is captured in Psalm 145:15,16 *"The eyes of all wait upon thee; and thou givest them their meat in due season. Thou openest thine hand, and satisfiest the desires of every living thing."* Note that God not only supplies human needs, but the needs of every living thing.

Whenever we become concerned about having our needs met, let us remember that we are parts of Him. In Acts 17:28 the Apostle Paul reminds us that we are positioned in God. While speaking to Athenian unbelievers, the Apostle Paul declared: *"For in him we live, and move, and have our being; as certain of your own poets have said, For we are also his offspring."* We are aware of how faithful most parents are in providing for their children. In Isaiah 49:15, God reminds us that He takes His parental responsibilities very seriously: *"Can a woman forget her suckling child, that she should not have compassion on the son of her womb? Yea, they may forget, yet will I not forget thee. Behold, I have graven thee upon the palms of my hands; thy walls are continually before me."*

It Is God Who Prays For Us

The extent to which God does everything for us is brought out by this interesting fact: we don't even know what to pray for, hence God prays for us. This truth that it is the Holy Spirit Who prays for us is declared in Romans 8:26,27:

> *Likewise the Spirit also helpeth our infirmities: for we know not what we should pray for as we ought: but the Spirit itself maketh intercession for us with groanings which cannot be uttered. And he that searcheth the heart knoweth what is the mind of the Spirit, because he maketh intercession for the saints according to the will of God.*

The fact that it is God Who does everything for mankind is supported by this statement Jesus made concerning our approach to God: *"Jesus saith unto him, I am the way, the truth and the life: no man cometh unto the Father, but by me."*

In conclusion, let us remember that we were never created to function as independent entities, but as dependent extensions of an Omnipotent God. His Divine love, mercy and grace made us become parts of Himself through our shared life with Jesus. In this context our dependence on God's pervasive involvement in our lives is geared to remove our human limitations. May we always recognize and voice that it is God Who must in all things work for us and through us.

CHAPTER 7

The Components of Ingratitude

The Scriptures teach that it is the goodness of God that leads us to repentance (Romans 2:4). We are aware that it is through repentance that our sins are forgiven. Failure to recognize, respond or to be grateful for God's goodness produces an unrepentant heart. Webster's Dictionary defines ingratitude as thanklessness and insensibility to kindness. Is ingratitude a sin? Note that thanklessness is mentioned in 2 Timothy 3:2 as among the sins of the last days: *"For men shall be lovers of themselves, covetous, boasters, proud, blasphemers, disobedient to parents, unthankful, unholy."*

When we carefully consider what sin is, we find that there is a link between ingratitude and every sin we commit. Had Lucifer and his followers been sufficiently grateful there would have been no room for the entrance of sin. What causes the human heart to become poisoned with ingratitude? Very often our urgent needs promote within us a spirit of ingratitude. We become ungrateful when a person who was kind to us before, fails to respond to our current urgent request. We can become so obsessed with what we require that we begin to think irrational thoughts. Such thoughts place little or no value on kindnesses previously received from a benefactor. We even begin to blame the benefactor for our present lack. We have a tendency to focus on what we don't have rather than those favors or blessings we received in the past.

My Own Experience With Urgent Needs

Several years ago while on an early morning walk, I found myself wondering why God was refusing to help me with a computer class assignment. I had prayed several times, did my research on the project and tried without success to obtain help from the instructor. It was a frustrating experience. It seemed to me that I was about to fail the course and God was up there in heaven sitting with His arms folded.

Suddenly, it dawned on me that my urgent need and my frustrations had drawn me into an attitude of discontent and ingratitude. When I came to myself, I immediately began to praise the Lord for all the help He had given me in the past. At the time I was attending Chubb Institute, a prestigious computer school in New York that taught computer programming. God brought to my attention that morning how He had previously influenced the instructor to give us a take home exam for a previous difficult course called JCL. With God's assistance I had passed that course with flying colors. A take home final exam was not the norm in that school. When I began to think logically I realized that God had brought me too far to abandon me. Needless to say the Lord intervened again on my behalf and I successfully completed the computer program at Chubb Institute.

The Adverse Effects of Urgent Needs

A situation in which an urgent need arises is the womb in which ingratitude develops. An ungrateful mind-set denies God's willingness to assist, and His power to produce results. Moreover, when we entertain an ungrateful spirit, we cannot enjoy peace of mind. Negative thoughts, blaming someone else and impending failure are what occupy the mind at the time. It is interesting that according to Philippians 4:6,7,19 God has made Himself responsible for supplying both our peace of mind and all our needs:

> Be careful for nothing; but in every thing by prayer and supplication with thanksgiving let your requests be made known unto God. And the peace of God, which passeth all understanding, shall keep your hearts and minds through Christ Jesus. But my God shall supply all your need according to his riches in glory by Christ Jesus.

When God says to be careful for nothing, He means that we must never worry and complain about anything, neither must we begin to blame others for our situation. Instead of blaming others, we must be consistently giving thanks to God as our primary source. Note that our requests must be made to God with thanksgiving. Other human beings may become the medium through whom God chooses to work, but they must never be considered our primary source of supply. For that reason, other people are not to be blamed for our lack. The more we keep blaming others, the more we are declaring that we are not depending totally on God.

When Job received the news that his possessions were stolen by the Sabeans and Chaldeans (Job 1:15,17), he refused to put the blame on men. Job recognized God as his only provider and protector. This important truth concerning our refusal to blame others for our lack is brought out in Job 1:21,22:

> *Then Job arose, and rent his mantle, and shaved his head, and fell down upon the ground, and worshipped, and said, Naked came I out of my mother's womb, and naked shall I return thither: the LORD gave, and the LORD hath taken away; blessed be the name of the Lord. In all this Job sinned not, nor charged God foolishly.*

Israel's Response to an Urgent Need for Food

Many of us have thought very poorly of the Israelites because of their frequent display of ingratitude and lack of faith in God. However, when we consider the urgent needs that confronted them in the vast wilderness, we ought to be more sympathetic. We need to remember that there were hundreds of little children crying for hunger. It is a difficult thing to see our children suffering. Exodus 16:3 relates the story of how the Israelites reacted when there was no food:

> *And the children of Israel said unto them, would to God we had died by the hand of the LORD in the land of Egypt, when we sat by the flesh pots, and when we did eat bread to the full; for ye have brought us forth into this wilderness, to kill this whole assembly with hunger.*

The urgent need for food certainly manifested in irrational thought processing. It may seem obvious to us that if God wanted to kill them, why would He deliver them from Egypt with several miracles? Did He not rain down plagues on the Egyptians to cause their deliverance? Why bring them so far into the wilderness, only to kill them in the end? Their irrational mindset should have disappeared when God eventually provided food. The incident is recalled in Exodus 16:4: "*Then said the LORD unto Moses, Behold, I will rain bread from heaven for you; and the people shall go out and gather a certain rate every day, that I may prove them, whether they will walk in my law, or not.*"

The Israelites' Urgent Need for Water

Not long after God showed His hand in providing food, there came the need for water. Did the Israelites learn from their last experience when God showed up and proved that His desire was not to kill them? Exodus 17:1,3 provide an account of how they responded to the urgent need for water: "... *and there was no water for the people to drink. And the people thirsted there for water; and the people murmured against Moses, and said, Wherefore is this that thou hast brought us up out of Egypt, to kill us and our children and our cattle with thirst?*" Exodus 17:4-6 relate that Moses cried out to God Who instructed Moses to strike the rock. Enough water came out of the rock to satisfy the thirst of everyone including the animals.

All the miracles that God had performed in the past were not sufficient to stir up their faith to wait patiently for His provision. We observe that Moses had not been troubled by the lack of water, but by the lack of trust exhibited by the people. In Exodus 17:2 Moses asks the question, "... *Why chide ye with me? Wherefore do ye tempt the LORD?*" The Israelites ought to have been building up their faith in God by focusing on all their advantages rather than what they lacked.

Wrong Focusing

Very often our ingratitude springs from our incorrect focus. Too often we focus on what we don't have rather than what we presently enjoy. In the Garden of Eden, the devil succeeded in changing the focus of Adam and Eve to something they felt they did not have. We all recognize that our ancestors, Adam and Eve, should have been happy and contented in their beautiful garden home. Satan suggested to the woman that there was something lacking in their lives that could make them happier—the forbidden fruit. The account of the interaction between Satan and Eve is found in Genesis 3:4-6:

> *And the serpent said unto the woman, Ye shall not surely die: For God doth know that in the day ye eat thereof, then your eyes shall be opened, and ye shall be as gods, knowing good and evil. And when the woman saw that the tree was good for food, and that it was pleasant to the eyes, and a tree to be desired to make one wise, she took of the fruit thereof, and did eat, and gave also unto her husband with her; and he did eat.*

Someone said that Eve swallowed Satan's lies, line, hook and sinker. Did she consider that she and her husband had been given the best that God could give? Doesn't God always give us His best? In Psalms 145:17 we are told: *"The LORD is righteous in all his ways, and holy in all his works."* Nothing flawed, nothing imperfect will God give to His beloved children. Today, modern man commits the same sin as Adam and Eve: we fail to place sufficient value on God's gifts to us. We are continually seeking happiness outside the box of obedience to God. The problem is that because we are imperfect and associate with others that are imperfect, we place God in the same category. If we had perfect trust in God we will never be guilty of ingratitude to Him.

In Hebrews 13:5,6 we are reminded to be content, to depend on God as our primary source:

> *Let your conversation be without covetousness; and be content with such things as ye have: for he hath said, I WILL NEVER LEAVE THEE, NOR FORSAKE THEE. So that we may boldly say, THE LORD IS MY HELPER, AND I WILL NOT FEAR WHAT MAN SHALL DO UNTO ME.*

To remain contented with all that God has given to us we need to guard our minds diligently. Within the mind lies the fuel that is used to spark the fires of discontent, ingratitude and sin. The Apostle Paul warns us in Philippians 4:8 about our mental focus:

> *Finally, brethren, whatsoever things are true, whatsoever things are honest, whatsoever things are just, whatsoever things are pure, whatsoever things are lovely, whatsoever things are of a good report; if there be any virtue, and if there be any praise, think on these things.*

Let us consider that the sin of Eve, the Israelites, Samson, David, Ananias and Sapphira and many others, all began with a discontented mindset. Be reminded that ingratitude is sparked by negative thoughts that must be replaced with thanksgiving.

Thanksgiving—A Divine Command

Thanksgiving is not an option that we choose to participate in when we feel good. Praise and thanksgiving are powerful offensive weapons that destroy the venom of ingratitude. In Ephesians 5:18-20 the Apostle Paul instructs us:

> *And be not drunk with wine, wherein is excess: but be filled with the Spirit; Speaking to yourselves in Psalms and hymns and spiritual songs, singing and making melody in your heart to the Lord; Giving thanks always for all things unto God and the Father in the name of our Lord Jesus Christ;*

The part of this Scripture that instructs us to give thanks always for everything reminds us of Job, who gave thanks even when he received severe bad news. David, who was a prolific composer of thanksgiving and worship Psalms supports the argument for consistent worship and praise. He declares in Psalm 107:21,22: *"Oh that men would praise the Lord for his goodness, and for his wonderful works to the children of men! And let them sacrifice the sacrifices of thanksgiving, and declare his works with rejoicing."*

Additionally, in Psalm 100:1,2,4 we are admonished to serve the Lord with gladness and offer up praise and thanksgiving: *"Make a joyful noise unto the LORD, all ye lands. Serve the LORD with gladness: come before his presence with singing. Enter into his gates with thanksgiving, and into his courts with praise: be thankful unto him, and bless his name."*

Praise and thanksgiving are necessary not only during times of peaceful situations, but especially in times of distress when we are faced with urgent needs. We are given an example in 2 Chronicles 20:21,22. Jehoshaphat, King of Judah and his people were vastly outnumbered and were about to be attacked by the Moabites and Ammonites. It was their singing and praise that preceded the destruction of their enemies by God. Here is the account of how King Jehoshaphat mobilized his people to praise God when faced with an urgent need:

> *And when he had consulted with the people, he appointed singers unto the LORD, and that should praise the beauty of holiness, as they went out before the army, and to say, Praise the LORD; for his mercy endureth for ever. And when they began to sing and to praise, the LORD set ambushments against the children of Ammon, Moab, and Mount Seir, which were come against Judah; and they were smitten.*

In conclusion, let us strive to defeat the sin of ingratitude. To do this our primary task must be to fill our minds continually with thanksgiving and praise to God for all His benefits. Secondly, we must apply adequate words and acts of appreciation to ascribe proper value for kindness and favors we receive from others. In addition, since human beings are not our primary source of benefits, let us refrain from blaming others for our lack. Let us like Job be totally dependent on God for all our needs.

CHAPTER 8

When God Disappears

When God seems to suddenly disappear
It is part of a Divine plan
You may yield to fear and sink in despair
If you do understand

These are the words of a song composed by the author several years ago. As the song indicates, there are indeed times in the life of every believer when God seems to disappear. This act of God is merely part of the process to build our faith while carrying out his purpose for us. God seemed to have disappeared from Joseph, from the children of Israel, from David, from Job, from Paul and even from Jesus. However, we are always rewarded for our troubles somewhere along the journey. Someone said that we receive double for our trouble. Job declared that we shall come forth like gold.

We Are Always Winners

Romans 8:28-32 (NLT) assures us that God is always involved in every minute detail of our lives including those trying seasons of distress when He seems to have disappeared. Moreover, God always rewards us by changing every evil thing into ultimate good:

> *And we know that God causes everything to work together for the good of those who love God and are called according to his purpose for them. For God knew his people in advance, and he chose them to become like his Son, so that his Son would be the first born among many brothers and sisters. And having chosen them, he called them to come to him. And having called them, he gave them right standing with himself. And having given them right standing, he gave them his glory.*

In this Scripture God is assuring us that nothing in the life of those who are in Christ could go wrong. He will cause every incident and every situation that affects us to work together for our good. Regardless of what happens to us, God has already predestinated that we come out of it as winners. This is indeed a fabulous Divine gift.

The win-win position that God gave us reminds me of a game we played as children. We would make a proposal by way of a bet to another person with the result to be determined by flipping a coin. We would say in a muffled tone quickly to the person, "head I win, tail you lose." The person to whom this was addressed would be instructed to choose one side of the coin before it was flipped. Obviously, regardless of which side of the coin that emerged on top, the one who made the proposal came out the winner. This reality that everything that happens to us works together for our good means that we will always come out winners. This is God's gift to His followers. Isn't it marvelous that even though we make mistakes (and we all do), God will change each mistake into something good? That's what God promises us.

Secondly, did you notice that God gave us right standing with Himself? How awesome it is that the great God of Heaven and earth is satisfied with us and glorifies us! We all crave acceptance from other human beings. The extent to which we have been accepted by God is expressed in Romans 8:33: *"Who dares accuse us whom God has chosen for his own? No one—for God himself has given us right standing with himself."* There ought to be no room in our lives for low self-esteem or depression. We are so special in God's sight that He is displeased with anyone who criticizes us. This truth is found in Isaiah 54:17:

> *No weapon that is formed against thee shall prosper; and every tongue that shall rise against thee in judgment thou shalt condemn. This is the heritage of the servants of the LORD, and their righteousness is of me, saith the LORD.*

All Things Worked For Joseph's Good

The problems faced by Joseph must have been terribly frustrating. The God who had given him dreams indicating that he had a bright future as a leader, seemed to have disappeared for several years. Not only was he sold by his brothers to become a slave. But he was subsequently wrongly

Dr. Grell Ferdinand

imprisoned by his master. He must have wondered why God disappeared. Psalms 105:17-21 provide a summary of what Joseph experienced:

> *He sent a man before them, even Joseph, who was sold for a servant: Whose feet they hurt with fetters: he was laid in iron: Until the time that his word came: the word of the Lord tried him. The king sent and loosed him; even the ruler of the people and let him go free. He made him lord of his house, and ruler of his substance:*

From the experience of Joseph we are made to understand that hurting is a normal part of the life of God's children on earth. Usually, whenever we are hurting we tend to think that our hurts are abnormal and that God has disappeared. However, hurting is part of the process of changing the metal into gold. Also, in the story of Joseph we learn that the Lord of the universe controls all the details including the time of release from prison into promotion. What is interesting about Joseph's experience is how his circumstances fitted into God's plan of bringing relief from famine to his father and his brothers. We need to always remember that God has a plan that is being worked out, which will ultimately bring us promotion and glory.

The Israelites Flunked Their Test

When the Israelites journeyed from Egypt to Canaan, they did not understand about trusting God when things get tough. For the short periods of time during which they had suffered from a lack of water and from a lack of food, God seemed to have disappeared. They did not believe that God had made Himself responsible for supplying all their needs. Their faith in God should have been built up since they had witnessed all of the miracles He performed to free them from Egyptian slavery. We could say that part of their problem was that they had a very short memory. Psalm 106:7,21, 24,25 summarize their rebellion and their failure to wait for His provision and deliverance:

> *Our fathers understood not thy wonders in Egypt; they remembered not the multitude of thy mercies; but provoked him at the sea, even at the Red sea. They forgat God their Saviour, which had done great things in Egypt. Yea, they despised the pleasant land, they believed not his word:*

But murmured in their tents, and hearkened not unto the voice of the LORD.

Job's Experience

Most of us are acquainted with the story of Job which begins with his family and himself growing in prosperity and enjoying Divine blessings. However, trouble struck suddenly as Satan took away his possessions, killed his children and engulfed his body with sickness. His declaration of deep trust when God seemed to have disappeared is captured in Job 1: 20-22:

> *Then Job arose, and rent his mantle, and shaved his head, and fell down upon the ground, and worshipped, and said, Naked came I out of my mother's womb, and naked shall I return thither: the LORD gave, and the LORD hath taken away; blessed be the name of the Lord. In all this Job sinned not, nor charged God foolishly.*

Ultimately, God healed his illness and rewarded him double for his troubles according to the record found in Job 42: 10, 12,13:

> *And the Lord turned the captivity of Job, when he prayed for his friends: and the LORD gave Job twice as much as he had before. So the LORD blessed the latter end of Job more than his beginning: for he had fourteen thousand sheep, and six thousand camels, and a thousand yoke of oxen, and a thousand she asses. He had also seven sons and three daughters.*

David's Experience

David loved the Lord and the Lord poured out His love and blessings upon David and even his descendants. However, there were several times when God seemed to have disappeared from David's view. On one occasion according to Psalms 13:1-3 David laments:

> *How long wilt thou forget me, O LORD? How long wilt thou hide thy face from me? How long shall I take counsel in my soul, having sorrow in my heart daily? How long shall mine enemy be exalted over me? Consider and hear me, O LORD my God: lighten mine eyes, lest I sleep the sleep of death;*

We remember that Samuel was instructed by God to anoint David as the king of Israel when he was still a young man (1 Samuel 16:13). Later on, after running away from Saul who tried to kill him, David hid in the forests with his men for several years. God seemed to have disappeared from view. Ultimately, David became king after Saul's death.

The problems of David did not end with his ascension to the throne. The record does not state that he lived happily ever after. During David's reign, his son, Absalom, rebelled, took over the throne and David was on the run again. The God who had finally exalted him as the king of all Israel, seemed to have disappeared again. However, David was ultimately restored to the throne after Absalom's death.

What should we do when God seems to disappear? We need to apply the reassuring words of David which are found in Psalms 37:5-7:

> Commit thy way unto the LORD; trust also in him; and he shall bring it to pass.
> And he shall bring forth thy righteousness as the light, and thy judgment as the noonday. Rest in the LORD, and wait patiently for him: fret not thyself because of him who prospereth in his way, because of the man who bringeth wicked devices to pass.

Did Jesus Ever Lose Sight Of His Father?

It is difficult for us to believe that the Father would put on what seemed like a disappearing act involving His beloved Son, Jesus. However, from the account found in Matthew 27:46 as Jesus hanged on the cross, He must have felt that He was abandoned:

> Now from the sixth hour there was darkness over all the land unto the ninth hour. And about the ninth hour Jesus cried with a loud voice, saying Eli, Eli, lama, sabachthani? That is to say, MY GOD, MY GOD, WHY HAST THOU FORSAKEN ME?

Was Jesus really abandoned? Never! In Hebrews 1:13, we learn how the Father subsequently exalted Jesus: *"But to which of the angels said he at any time, SIT ON MY RIGHT HAND, UNTIL I MAKE THINE ENEMIES THY FOOTSTOOL?"*

Paul Shares His Experiences

The Apostle Paul was no stranger to problems. He must have wondered many times why God seemed so distant. In 2 Corinthians 11:24-27 Paul tells of some of his experiences when God seemed to have disappeared:

> *Of the Jews five times received I forty stripes save one. Thrice was I beaten with rods, once was I stoned, thrice I suffered shipwreck, a night and a day I have been in the deep; In journeyings often, in perils of waters, in perils of robbers, in perils by mine own countrymen, in perils by heathen, in perils in the city, in perils in the wilderness, in perils in the sea, in perils among false brethren; in weariness and painfulness, in watchings often, in hunger and thirst, in fastings often, in cold and nakedness.*

The Apostle Paul did not suffer in vain. He was certain of his rewards. Here is his testimony found in 2 Timothy 4:7,8:

> *I have fought a good fight, I have finished my course, I have kept the faith: Henceforth there is laid up for me a crown of righteousness, which the Lord, the righteous judge, shall give me at that day: and not to me only, but unto all them also that love his appearing.*

We Must Never Fear

How can a person endure severe problems and still remain faithful to God? The Apostle Paul's experiences must teach us that since God never abandons us, we must become fearless. A very frequent command that God gives to us in His Word is to have no fear. In Luke 12:7 (NLT) we are told, *"And the very hairs of on your head are all numbered. So don't be afraid; you are more valuable to God than a whole flock of sparrows."* God's concern for us and His control of every circumstance in our lives is revealed in Mark 4:37-41 (NLT) where an incident took place with Jesus and His disciples while they were in a boat crossing a lake:

> *But soon a fierce storm came up. High waves were breaking into the boat, and it began to fill with water. Jesus was sleeping at the back of the boat with his head on a cushion. The disciples woke him up, shouting, "Teacher, don't you care that we're going to drown?" When Jesus woke up, he rebuked the wind and said to the waves, "Silence! Be still!" Suddenly*

the wind stopped, and there was a great calm. Then he asked them, "Why are you afraid? Do you still have no faith?" The disciples were absolutely terrified. "Who is this man?" they asked each other. "Even the wind and waves obey him!"

We Must Avoid Judging Others

There is a natural tendency among many of us to view problems as punishment by God for iniquities. However, neither Joseph, the Israelites, Job, David, the Apostle Paul nor Jesus was being punished by God for their sins. Instead, God fitted their problems into His Divine plan to bless both themselves and others. In the case of the man who was blind from birth, the disciples of Jesus questioned whether the blindness was judgment from God for sins committed. The response from Jesus found in John 9:2,3 is very enlightening: *"And his disciples asked him, saying, Master, who did sin, this man, or his parents, that he was born blind? Jesus answered, Neither hath this man sinned, nor his parents: but that the works of God should be made manifest in him."*

We learn from this episode that we must be careful about judging each other. God is also displeased when we "bad mouth or bad talk" others. Did you know that the Holy Angels are not allowed to speak evil of Satan? This is brought out in Jude 1:9 (NLT): *"But even Michael, one of the mightiest of the angels, did not dare accuse the devil of blasphemy, but simply said, "The Lord rebuke you!" (This took place when Michael was arguing with the devil about Moses' body.)"*

Additionally, we have been warned in Titus 3:2, *"To speak evil of no man, to be no brawlers, but gentle, shewing all meekness unto all men."*

In conclusion, let us not be discouraged as troubles come our way. When God seems to disappear, let us wait patiently on our Heavenly Father for deliverance. Here is what God says about troubles in Psalms 34:17, *"The righteous cry, and the LORD heareth, and delivereth them out of all their troubles."*

CHAPTER 9

God Calls Us to Bless Us and to Bless Others Through Us

And the Spirit and the bride say, Come. And let him that heareth say, Come. And let him that is athirst come. And whosoever will, let him take the water of life freely Revelation 21:17.

When God calls us to come to Him, His purpose is first of all to bless us and also to bless others through us. Without exception God calls everyone and each of us has a choice to make. If we accept His Divine invitation He guarantees us a destiny of an abundant and superior lifestyle. If we reject His call we will experience a life of failure and ultimate eternal destruction. Before the creation of the world, God anticipated the entrance of sin and took on the responsibility of cleansing us from all filthiness. In this context God called Jesus to become the sin bearer and to provide an example of service to others. Following the entrance of sin, Adam and Eve, Abraham, David, Moses, the twelve disciples of Jesus and people in every generation including ours are given the choice of accepting or rejecting God's call.

God Calls Us to Remove Barriers to Our Blessings

Note that sin is like a hurricane. It not only brings death and destruction but makes the roads impassable and difficult for aid to be brought in. The result of sin's power to separate us from our Divine benefactor is expressed in Isaiah 59:1,2:

> *BEHOLD, the LORD'S hand is not shortened, that it cannot save; neither is his ear heavy, that it cannot hear: But your iniquities have separated between you and your God, and your sins have hid his face from you, that he will not hear. And judgment is turned away backward, and justice standeth afar off: for truth is fallen in the street, and equity cannot enter.*

Sin deprives us of God's presence and the abundant blessings He so much desires to pour out upon us. God's urgent call to us to allow Him to clear the debris of sin from our lives is revealed in Isaiah 1:18-20:

> Come now, and let us reason together, saith the LORD: though your sins be as scarlet, they shall be as white as snow; though they be red as crimson, they shall be as wool. If ye be willing and obedient, ye shall eat the good of the land: But if ye refuse and rebel, ye shall be devoured with the sword: for the mouth of the LORD hath spoken it.

The Parable of the Great Supper

Perhaps the clearest declaration of God's generous invitation to every one of us in order to pour out His blessings upon us is found in the parable of the Great Supper told by Jesus. The call to come and be blessed is declared in Luke 14:16,17: "*Then said he unto him, A certain man made a great supper and bade many: And sent his servant at supper time to say to them that were bidden, Come; for all things are now ready.*" Note that it was called "a great supper." Obviously, this was not an ordinary meal prepared by an ordinary person. It must have been a feast involving lavish expenditure with delicacies specially prepared to please the invitees. To host such a great supper the owner had to be both generous and rich in resources.

Unfortunately, this well intentioned lord with all his generous preparation and invitation was greeted with contempt. Luke 14:18-20 records the people's response:

> And they all with one consent began to make excuse. The first said unto him, I have bought a piece of ground, and I must needs go and see it: I pray thee have me excused. And another said, I have bought five yoke of oxen, and I go to prove them: I pray thee have me excused. And another said, I have married a wife, and therefore I cannot come.

This parable provides a graphic description of (a) the Father's heart of love and generosity (b) the human heart of unwillingness to receive the bounties that God desires to give us (c) our lame excuses for refusing the Divine invitation. Incidentally, it is interesting that our excuses for refusing the invitation may seem to be very legitimate in our own eyes, but certainly not so in God's eyes. Note also that fortunately for us God did not abandon the world in disgust, but continued patiently to reach out. As one songwriter puts it, "He looked beyond our faults and saw our need." Luke 14:21,23 describes God's patient perseverance in well doing:

> *So the servant came, and shewed his lord these things. Then the master of the house being angry said to his servant, Go out quickly into the streets and lanes of the city, and bring in hither the poor, and maimed, and the halt, and the blind. And the lord said unto the servant, go out into the highways and hedges, and compel them to come in, that my house may be filled.*

Aren't you glad that God did not give up but persisted in His invitations to all of us? In contrast how much patience do we display in dealing with stubborn unbelievers?

God's Call Upon Jesus

Hebrews 10:4-7 records the agreement of Jesus to God's call to go down to earth as a living sacrifice for the sins of mankind. Animal sacrifices were merely symbolic of the true cleansing performed by the Lamb of God which took away the sin of the world:

> *For it is not possible that the blood of bulls and of goats should take away sins. Wherefore when he cometh into the world, he saith, SACRIFICE AND OFFERING THOU WOULDEST NOT, BUT A BODY HAST THOU PREPARED ME: IN BURNT OFFERINGS AND SACRIFICES FOR SIN THOU HAST HAD NO PLEASURE. THEN SAID I, LO, I COME (IN THE VOLUME OF THE BOOK IT IS WRITTEN OF ME,) TO DO THY WILL, O GOD.*

We are very fortunate that Jesus obeyed the call to rescue us. We know that it was a successful mission because His accomplishments are recorded in Isaiah 53:4-6:

> *Surely he hath borne our griefs, and carried our sorrows: yet we did esteem him stricken, smitten of God, and afflicted. But he was wounded for our transgressions, he was bruised for our iniquities: the chastisement of our peace was upon him; and with his stripes we are healed. All we like sheep*

have gone astray; we have turned everyone to his own way: and the LORD hath laid on him the iniquity of us all.

Isaiah 53:12 describes how the Father rewarded Jesus for His obedience to the call: *"Therefore will I divide him a portion with the great, and he shall divide the spoil with the strong; because he hath poured out his soul unto death: and he was numbered with transgressors; and he bare the sin of many, and made intersession for the transgressors."*

God Called Adam and Eve

After they had sinned in the Garden of Eden, Adam and Eve went into hiding. According to Genesis 3:8,9,15 God did not abandon them, but instead called them, forgave them and provided hope:

And they heard the voice of the LORDG walking in the garden in the cool of the day: and Adam and his wife hid themselves from the presence of the LORD God amongst the trees of the garden. And the LORD God called unto Adam, and said unto him, Where art thou?" To the serpant God said: *"And I will put enmity between thee and the woman, and between thy seed and her seed; it shall bruise thy head, and thou shalt bruise his heel.*

Abraham's Call

Abraham's experience serves as a good example of what is offered to every one of us. Genesis 12:1-4 provides the detail of God's call to Abraham:

Now the LORD had said unto Abram, Get thee out of thy country, and from thy kindred, and from thy father's house, unto a land that I will shew thee: And I will make of thee a great nation, and I will bless thee, and make thy name great; and thou shalt be a blessing: And I will bless them that bless thee, and curse him that curseth thee: and in thee shall all families of the earth be blessed.

Although this may seem to be a personal call directed to Abraham, the basic content of the message is directed to each one of us. (1) Since the spiritual, moral and physical environment in which Abraham lived would restrict the tremendous vision that God had in mind for him, he was commanded to get out of there. We too are ordered by God to change our evil ways and allow Him to guide us. (2) In addition, because Abraham had no idea where he was going or how to get there, he had to be completely dependent on God: he had to walk by faith and not by sight. In 2 Corinthians 5:7 we are instructed to walk by faith and not by sight. (3) It was God's responsibility not only to provide detailed directions but to ensure that he got there safely. In Psalm 32:8 God says to us: *"I will instruct thee and teach in the way which thou shalt go: I will guide thee with mine eye."* (4) The blessings he would receive were to be shared with others. God told him: *"thou shalt be a blessing;"* In Isaiah 60:1-4 we are also told:

> *ARISE, shine: for thy light is come, and the glory of the LORD is risen upon thee. For, behold, the darkness shall cover the earth, and gross darkness the people: But the LORD shall arise upon thee, and his glory shall be seen upon thee. And the Gentiles shall come to thy light, and kings to the brightness of thy rising.*

Note that God made Himself responsible for protecting Abraham. When Pharaoh attempted to take away Sarah, Abraham's wife (although it was done in ignorance), God showed up and worked miracles to set her free: *"And the Lord plagued Pharaoh and his house with great plagues because of Sarai Abraham's wife. And Pharoah commanded his men concerning him: and they sent him away, and his wife, and all that he had."*

Abraham's Acceptance of God's Call Resulted in Riches

This truth that God calls us in order to bless us is demonstrated in His dealings with Abraham. Note, however, that God called him to move out of his environment. Similarly in order to bless us, God usually calls for changes in our attitude and behavior. The Apostle Paul had to make changes in his program. In his defense before King Agrippa, he explained that he obeyed God's call: *"Whereupon, O king Agrippa, I was not disobedient unto the heavenly vision."*

When Abraham obeyed God's instruction to leave his relatives and set out for the unknown land, God rewarded him. Genesis 13:5,6 declare: *"And Lot also, which was with Abraham, had flocks, and herds, and tents. And the land was not able to bear them, that they might dwell together: for their substance was great, so that they could not dwell together."* In addition,

Genesis 13:2 confirms that God had indeed blessed Abraham: *"And Abraham was very rich in cattle, in silver, and in gold."*

Isaiah Agreed to God's Call

According to Isaiah 6:1 the prophet Isaiah had a vision of heaven which scared him: *"In the year that king Uzziah died I saw also the Lord sitting upon a throne, high and lifted up, and his train filled the temple. Above it stood the seraphims: each one had six wings; with twain he covered his face, and with twain he covered his feet, and with twain he did fly."*

When Isaiah voiced his unworthiness and dismay over what he had seen, one of the seraphims provided a solution as recorded in Isaiah 6:7,8: *"Then flew one of the seraphims unto me, having a live coal in his hand, which he had taken with the tongs from off the alter: And he laid it upon my mouth, and said, Lo, this hath touched thy lips: and thy iniquity is taken away, and thy sin purged."*

Isaiah 6:8 also reveals God's call to Isaiah and his agreement to become a mouthpiece for God: *"Also I heard the voice of the Lord, saying, Whom shall I send, and who will go for us? Then said I, Here am I: send me."* These words ought to be everybody's response to God's call upon our lives.

CHAPTER 10

Our Father is a Superfluous God

More sky than man can see
More sea than he can sail
More sun than he can bear to watch
More stars than he can scale
More breath than he can breathe
More yield than he can sow
More grace than he can comprehend
More love than he can know

Anonymous

This poem expresses very beautifully the truth regarding the superfluity of our Creator. Our Loving Heavenly Father certainly must have originated the concept of superfluity which signifies excessive abundance or more than enough. This idea of an overly generous God is expressed in Ephesians 3:20: *"Now unto him that is able to do exceeding abundantly above all that we ask or think, according to the power that worketh in us . . ."*

Since God Who existed from eternity has always been extremely generous in His dealings with mankind, it would seem that the human definition of '*superfluity*' found in the Webster's Dictionary was borrowed from God's Word. Here is how it is defined: *"Exceeding what is needed; excessively abundant; surplus."* We see this Divine principle being employed in the salvation process, in God's provision for the Israelites in the Wilderness, in His provision for Abraham, in God's gifts to Solomon, in the feeding of the five thousand by Jesus and many other incidents mentioned in the Bible.

The Superfluity of Salvation

In the salvation process, we see the principle of superfluity at work as we examine the tremendous difference between our prior sinful and rebellious condition and the very generous promotion given to us by God. Ephesians 2:2 (Amplified) describes our previous abysmal state before we were saved:

> *In which at one time you walked [habitually]. You were following the course and fashion of this world [were under the sway of the tendency of this present age], following the prince of the power of the air. [You were obedient to and under the control of] the [demon] spirit that still constantly works in the sons of disobedience [the careless, the rebellious, and the unbelieving, who go against the purpose of God].*

No one would expect the sinful people described above to even escape their seemingly hopeless condition. However, not only did God rescue human beings from a destiny of doom and destruction, but promoted us to share the life and the inheritance of His Son, Jesus. Listen to this Divine principle of superfluity in action in Ephesians 2:4,5,6 (Amplified):

> *But God—so rich is He in mercy! Because of and in order to satisfy the great and wonderful and intense love with which He loved us, Even when we were dead (slain) by [our own shortcomings and trespasses, He made us alive together in fellowship and in union with Christ; [He gave us the very life of Christ Himself, the same new life with which He quickened Him, for] it is by grace (His favor and mercy which you did not deserve) that you are saved (delivered from judgment and made partakers of Christ's salvation), and He raised us up together with Him and made us sit down together [giving us joint seating with Him] in the heavenly sphere [by virtue of our being] in Christ Jesus (the Messiah, the Anointed One).*

From being dead in trespasses and sins to a position of joint seating with Christ is certainly a display of superfluity on God's part. In Romans 8:17 we are called joint-heirs with Christ: *"And if children, then heirs, heirs of God, and joint-heirs with Christ . . ."*

God's Superfluous Gifts to Abraham

First of all, to think that God actually regarded Abraham as righteous simply because he believed God. This fact is supported in Genesis 15:6: *"And he believed in the Lord and he counted it to him for righteousness."* This generosity of God is supported in Romans 4:2,3: *"For if Abraham were justified by works, he hath whereof to glory; but not before God. For what saith the scripture? ABRAHAM BELIEVED GOD, AND IT WAS COUNTED UNTO HIM FOR RIGHTEOUSNESS.* " In addition to the very generous exchange of awarding righteousness for faith, God blessed Abraham with more than enough wealth as expressed in Genesis 13:2: *"And Abraham was very rich in cattle, in silver, and in gold. "*

The Israelites Experienced God's Abundance

When the Israelites murmured impatiently in the wilderness because of a lack of food, God sent more meat than they needed in the evening and so much manna every morning that they could not resist the temptation to hoard some for their future use. God's over abundant supply is recorded in Exodus 16:13,35: *"And it came to pass, that at even the quails came up, and covered the camp: and in the morning the dew lay round about the host. And the children of Israel did eat manna forty years, until they came to a land inhabited; they did eat manna, until they came unto the borders of the land of Canaan."*

God Gave Solomon Excessive Abundance

God's excessive abundance given to Solomon is described in 1 Kings 10:14-17:

> *Now the weight of gold that came to Solomon in one year was six hundred three score and six talents of gold ($3.83 billion), Beside that he had of the merchantmen, and of the traffick of the spice merchants, and of all the kings of Arabia, and other governors of the country. And king Solomon made two hundred targets of beaten gold: six hundred shekels of gold went one target ($3,840,000). And he made three hundred shields of beaten gold; three pounds of gold went to one shield: and the king put them in the house of the forest of Lebanon.*

Superfluity In Action When Jesus Fed Thousands

The concept of Divine superfluity is dramatically portrayed when Jesus fed a multitude of men, women and children on two occasions. The first episode is recorded in Matthew 14:19-21:

And he commanded the multitude to sit down on the grass, and took the five loaves, and two fishes, and looking up to heaven, he blessed, and brake, and gave the loaves to his disciples, and the disciples to the multitude. And they did all eat, and were filled: and they took up of the fragments that remained twelve baskets full. And they that had eaten were about five thousand men, beside women and children.

The question could be asked, why didn't God provide just enough to feed the five thousand? To feed five thousand men beside women and children with five loaves and two fishes is sufficient evidence of Divine power. Why the extra fragments amounting to twelve baskets full? The only logical answer is that characteristically God is superfluous. We recall that Webster's dictionary defines superfluous as "Exceeding what is needed; excessively abundant; surplus."

A Superfluous Amount of Fish

This amazing account of Jesus' involvement with an abundance of fish caught by the Disciples is recorded in Luke 5:4,5: "*Now when he had left speaking, he said unto Simon, Launch out into the deep, and let down your nets for a draught.*" Peter protested because they had tried all night and had toiled without success. However, he agreed to try again to be obedient to his master. Luke 5:6,7 records the superfluous catch of fish:

And when they had this done, they inclosed a great multitude of fishes: and their net brake. And they beckoned unto their partners, which were in the other ship, that they should come and help them. And they came, and filled both the ships, so that they began to sink.

Wow! In order for the two boats to begin to sink there must have been a whole lot of fish in the two ships. That's the God we are describing—Jesus is introducing us to a more than enough God!

You Do Not Have Because You Do Not Ask

Have we been misunderstanding God's willingness to bestow upon us more than enough? Have we because of our ignorance been asking for just enough instead of more than enough? Since our Heavenly Father is a superfluous God He expects us to ask for more than we have been asking for. This thought is brought in James 4:2 (Amplified): . . . "*You do not have because you do not ask.*"

This truth that we need to ask for more than we usually do is supported by the account found in 2 Kings 13:18,19. Just before his death, Elisha commanded Jehoahaz, King of Judah to take some arrows and strike them on the ground. This act of striking the arrows on the ground was very significant because it represented the extent that the kingdom of Judah would be successful against her enemy, Syria. Elisha was annoyed because the King ought to have done more as the following Scripture suggests:

> *And he said, Take the arrows. And he took them. And he said unto the king of Israel, Smite upon the ground. And he smote thrice and stayed. And the man of God was wroth with him, and said, Thou shouldest have smitten five or six times; then hast thou smitten Syria till thou hadst consumed it: whereas thou shalt smite Syria but thrice.*

Could it be that we have failed to accomplish more because we anticipate little? Do we now understand that God is a more than enough God? Remember God is able to do exceeding abundantly more than we ask or think.

CHAPTER 11

With All Your Heart

The human heart is the seat of all love, emotion and passion. Passion is described in Webster's Dictionary as *intense or overpowering emotion*; and *as an eager outreaching of the mind toward some special object.* Our Heavenly Father loves all His children passionately and demonstrated His love for us with the ultimate gift, the gift of His Son. God's intense love demand's a passionate response from us. The entire history of mankind is characterized by our rebellion against our Creator and our lukewarm response to His intense love.

God's Passion Expressed by Giving His All

Let us review some Scriptures that declare God's passionate love for us. Romans 8:32 declares: *"He that spared not his own Son, but delivered him up for us all, how shall he not with him also freely give us all things?"* God is willing to give us all things? That is exactly what the word says.

The extent of this Divine love is also expressed in Jeremiah 31:3: *"The Lord hath appeared of old unto me, saying, Yea, I have loved thee with an everlasting love: therefore with lovingkindness have I drawn thee."* Note that God has been expressing His love for us 'of old,' meaning a long time ago. Also, be aware that God's love is not merely expressed in words but in His kindness to us. This kindness has been manifested in the giving of His Son as declared in John 3:16: *"For God so loved the world, that he gave his only begotten son , that whosoever believeth in him should not perish, but have everlasting life."*

The Son of God exchanged places with every human being by becoming sin for all of us so that we would receive reconciliation with His Father and be considered righteous in His sight. This powerful manifestation of love is also declared in 2 Corinthians 5:21: *"For he hath made him to be sin for us, who knew no sin; that we might be made the righteousness of God in him."*

God Laments Our Lukewarm State

In Revelation 3:15-18 God expresses His displeasure with our lack of passion which is equated with lukewarmness: *"I know thy works, that thou art neither cold nor hot: I would thou wert cold or hot. So then because thou art lukewarm, and neither cold nor hot, I will spue thee out of my mouth."*

In addition, God talks about our rebellion against Him. Isaiah 1:3,4 captures God's heart as He laments our unresponsiveness to His love: *"Hear, O heavens, and give ear, O earth: for the LORD hath spoken, I have nourished and brought up children, and they have rebelled against me."* God's enemy, Satan, has successfully seduced human beings with a multitude of distractions. As a result, we have become so busy and engaged in trivialities that we place God on the back burner of our lives. Only a fervent search for God, a willingness to put aside distractions, and an eagerness to serve Him passionately will yield a successful relationship with Him. In Jeremiah 29:13 God expresses the quality of response He desires from us: *"And ye shall seek me, and find me, when ye shall search for me with all your heart."*

David's Passion for God

King David loved God passionately and expressed it repeatedly in the Psalms. In Psalm 55:17 he said, *"Evening and morning, and at noon, will I pray, and cry aloud: and he shall hear my voice."* David's deep desire for God, his fervent search for Him and his frequent times of worship are also captured in Psalm 63:1-4,6:

> *O GOD, thou art my God; early will I seek thee: my soul thirsteth for thee, my flesh longeth for thee in a dry and thirsty land, where no water is; To see thy power and thy glory, so as I have seen thee in the sanctuary. Because thy lovingkindness is better than life, my lips shall praise thee. Thus will I bless thee while I live I will lift up my hands in thy name. When I remember thee upon my bed, and meditate on thee in the night watches.*

Although his kingly responsibilities must have been urgent, notice how David frequently put aside every distraction in order to focus on the Lord.

2 Samuel 6:14,15 recounts the story of the ark being brought into the city of David. Note how David displayed his delight by dancing passionately before the Lord: *"And David danced before the LORD with all*

his might; and David was girded with a linen ephod. So David and all the house of Israel brought up the ark of the LORD with shouting, and with the sound of the trumpet."

Michal, Saul's daughter, one of David's wives, was filled with contempt for David's display. In 2 Samuel 6:16 we read: "*And as the ark of the Lord came into the city of David, Michal Saul's daughter looked through the window, and saw king David leaping and dancing before the LORD; and she despised him in her heart.*"

Later, as the opportunity arose when David came home, she criticized him because she said that he "*. . . uncovered himself to day in the eyes of the handmaids of his servants, as one of the vain fellows shamelessly uncovereth himself.*" Note, however, that God was pleased with David's display and, in fact, showed His displeasure with Michal for in 2 Samuel 6:23 we read: "*Therefore Michal the daughter of Saul had no child unto the day of her death.*"

The Passionate Widow and the Mite

God demonstrated His great love for us by giving us His Son. Our fervent love for God can also be demonstrated by our giving. Since we were created in God's image and likeness (Genesis 1:26,27), we must strive to resemble God in our generosity.

In Luke 21:3,4 Jesus took the time to focus the attention of His disciples on the sacrifice and generosity of a poor widow woman who placed in the offering plate everything she owned: "*And he said , Of a truth I say unto you, that this poor widow hath cast in more than they all: For all these have of their abundance cast in unto the offerings of God: but she of her penury hath cast in all the living that she had.*" She did not cast in quantitatively more than those who were rich, but she gave all her living—everything she owned. When we give our best to God it always catches His attention and God has promised to reward us according to Luke 6:38: "*Give, and it shall be given unto you; good measure, pressed down, and shaken together, and running over, shall men give unto your bosom. For with the same measure that ye mete withal it shall be measured to you again.*"

The Rich Young Ruler

The intensity and generosity of the widow woman serve as a contrast to the rich young ruler's lack of generosity. Luke 18:18-23 relates the dialogue between Jesus and the Rich Young Ruler who lacked the passion that God requires from His followers:

And a certain ruler asked him, saying, Good Master, what shall I do to inherit eternal life?" Jesus replied, "Thou knowest the commandments, Do NOT COMIT ADULTERY, DO NOT KILL, DO NOT STEAL, DO NOT BEAR FALSE WITNESS, HONOUR THY FATHER AND THY MOTHER. And he said, all these have I kept from my youth up. And when Jesus heard these things, he said unto him, "yet lackest thou one thing: sell all that thou has, and distribute unto the poor, and thou shalt have treasure in heaven."

This young man must seem in the eyes of most of us to be a very good man, for he had kept the commandments from his youth. However, he did not have the fervency and passion required for the kingdom. The poor widow gave her all but the rich young ruler refused to give his all. He was a lukewarm person. Lukewarm individuals do not give sacrificially. They give as little as they can. That extra, that sacrifice, that all which God requires is regarded by many persons as too much.

The Passion Of The Early Church

According to the words of a song composed by the author:

The Early Church met daily in the temple
Breaking bread from house to house as out example
They witnessed signs and wonders God's Spirit was outpoured
They put aside distractions and focused on the Lord

The words of this song were inspired by the Scripture found in Acts 2:46: *"And they continued daily with one accord in the temple, and breaking bread from house to house, did eat their meal with gladness and singleness of heart, Praising God, and having favor with all the people. And the Lord added to the church daily such as should be saved."*

Before the resurrection and the day of Pentecost, the entire group of disciples could have been characterized as fearful and faithless. However, Those disciples were transformed into bold, passionate, productive ambassadors after the resurrection of Jesus and the outpouring of the

Holy Ghost on the day of Pentecost. Acts 2:1-4 provide details of what transpired:

> *And when the day of Pentecost was fully come, they were all with one accord in one place. And suddenly there came a sound from heaven as of a rushing mighty wind, and it filled all the house where they were sitting. And there appeared unto them cloven tongues like as of fire, and it sat upon each of them. And they were all filled with the Holy Ghost, and began to speak with other tongues, as the Spirit gave them utterance.*

The entire account recorded in Acts chapter 2 shows that God had carefully prepared the setting and the foundation of the early church. It was no coincidence that according to the record on the day of Pentecost there were in Jerusalem Jews and devout men from every nation under heaven. God had marshaled them and positioned them to become participants of the early Church. They heard of the strange happenings and rushed to the place where the strange sounds originated. They were in time to hear Peter explain that God was accomplishing a new thing in their life time. This new thing had been prophesied by the prophet Joel many years before:

> *But Peter, standing up with the eleven, lifted up his voice, and said unto them, Ye men of Judaea, and all ye that dwell at Jerusalem, be this known unto you, and hearken to my words: For these are not drunken, as ye suppose, seeing it is but the third hour of the day. But this is that which was spoken by the prophet Joel; AND IT SHALL COME TO PASS IN THE LAST DAYS, SAITH GOD, I WILL POUR OUT OF MY SPIRIT UPON ALL FLESH: AND YOUR SONS AND YOUR DAUGHTERS SHALL PROPHESY, AND YOUR YOUNG MEN SHALL SEE VISIONS, AND YOUR OLD MEN SHALL DREAM DREAMS.*

Peter continued his address in Acts 2:32,33 by introducing Jesus as the physical descendant of David and as the Person about Whom David had prophesied: *"This Jesus hath God raised up, whereof we are all witnesses. Therefore being by the right hand of God exalted, and having received of the Father the promise of the Holy Ghost, he hath shed forth this, which ye now see and hear."*

According to the record found in Acts 2:37,38,41, Peter's address was met with enthusiastic response:

Now when they heard this, they were pricked in their heart, and said unto Peter and to the rest of the apostles Men and brethren, what shall we do? Then Peter said unto them, Repent, and be baptized every one of you in the name of Jesus Christ for the remission of sins, and ye shall receive the gift of the Holy Ghost. Then they that gladly received his word were baptized: and the same day there were added unto them about three thousand souls.

The early believers served with such passion that they made great sacrifices of their time and their monetary resources. Their enthusiasm is captured in Acts 2:46: *"And they, continuing daily with one accord in the temple, and breaking bread from house to house, did eat their meat with gladness and singleness of heart."*

After God used Peter and John to heal the man who had been lame from birth, a crowd gathered curious to find out how the man was healed. Of course, Peter took the opportunity to explain that it was Jesus who performed the miracle. The religious leaders were angry that the people were being taught about Jesus according to Acts 4:1-3:

And as they spake unto the people, the priests, and the captain of the temple, and the Sadducees, came upon them, Being grieved that they taught the people, and preached through Jesus the resurrection from the dead. And they laid hands on them, and put them in hold unto the next day: for it was now eventide.

The next day Annas, the high priest, Caiaphas, John, Alexander and others listened to Peter as he explained that the miracle was done in the name of Jesus: *"Be it known unto you all, and to all the people of Israel, that by the name of Jesus Christ of Nazareth, whom ye crucified, whom God raised from the dead, even by him doth this man stand before you whole."*

Peter and John refused to be intimidated by those austere Jewish leaders. The passion and boldness of the Apostles are expressed in their response in Acts 4:18-20:

And they called them, and commanded them not to speak at all nor teach in the name of Jesus. But Peter and John answered and said unto them, whether it be right in the sight of God to hearken unto you more than unto God, judge ye. For we cannot but speak the things which we have seen and heard.

According to Acts 2:44,45 the Early Church demonstrated their passion for God by their willingness to give to God not only their time but their possessions: *"And all that believed were together, and had all things common; And sold their possessions and goods, and parted them to all men, as every man had need."* In addition, Acts 4:36,37 provides detailed example of a passionate giver named Joses: *"And Joses, who by the Apostles was surnamed Barnabas, (which is, being interpreted, the son of consolation,) a Levite and of the country of Cyprus, Having land, sold it, and brought the money, and laid it at the apostles' feet."*

The Modern Church Criticized For Lack Of Passion

That God delights in our fervency, but repudiates our lukewarm state is clearly shown in his message to the Laodicean church in Revelation 3:14-18:

> *And unto the angel of the church of the Laodiceans write; These things saith the Amen, the faithful and true witness, the beginning of the creation of God; I know thy works, that thou art neither cold nor hot: I would thou wert cold or hot. So then because thou art lukewarm, and neither cold nor hot, I will spue thee out of my mouth.*

In conclusion, let us be aware that God is passionate and requires passionate relationships with us. Our love and devotion to God together with our passionate care for one another must always characterize us and never fall short.

CHAPTER 12

The Great Escape

The Holy Bible is replete with numerous accounts of divinely led human escapes. In addition to the many people who God delivered from bodily harm, even more importantly, there is an infinite number of saved individuals, who escaped the threat of God's wrath and destruction in hell's inferno. The goal of this sermon is to present a few examples of God's passion for providing great escapes from physical dangers and also from sin and its results.

The tremendous difference between the devils purpose to destroy and God's passion to provide escape is declared in John 10:10 (NLT): *"The thief's purpose is to steal and kill and destroy. My purpose is to give them a rich and satisfying life."* Every Divine promise and each requirement God gives us is geared to provide us with a rich and satisfying life and to help us escape destruction.

It is in this context that Psalm 124:7 declares: *"Our soul is escaped as a bird out of the snare of the fowlers: the snare is broken, and we are escaped."* This testimony penned by the Psalmist, David, could well be voiced by all of us who rejoice in the freedom effected by our Lord Jesus.

Among those who at some stage in their lives experienced miraculous escape from earthly harm were Noah and his family from the flood, Lot from the flames of Sodom, Sarah from the sexual advances of King Abimelech, the Israelites from Egyptian slavery, Queen Esther and her Jewish people from complete anihilation, Shadrach, Meshach and AbedNego from the fiery furnace, Daniel from the lion's den, Jesus' deliverance from stoning, Paul and Silas from prison and several others.

Noah Escapes the Flood

During the time of Noah, the earth was full of wickedness. God told Noah, the only righteous man on the earth, to build an ark, and preach to earth's inhabitants to repent and find safety in the ark. Since the people of Noah's day were not accustomed to rain, they despised Noah's warning. Genesis 7:11,17 (NLT) provide some details of the flood:

> *When Noah was 600 years old, on the seventeenth day of the second month, all the underground waters erupted from the earth, and the rain fell in mighty torrents from the sky. For forty days the floodwaters grew deeper, covering the ground and lifting the boat high above the earth. As the waters rose higher and higher above the ground, the boat floated safely on the surface.*

There was water everywhere. Of course, the people began to take notice and probably said to each other, "It seems that that crazy old man was not so crazy after all. Let's all head for the ark." But it was too late. God had shut the door of the ark. Only those inside the ark experienced the great escape.

God Delivered Sarah from King Abimilech

There was a time on earth when if you were blessed with a pretty wife, your life was in danger. Abraham lived during that time and he had a pretty wife. He advised her to inform others that she was his sister. Sarah caught King Abimelech's attention and he fetched her into his palace to join his harem of wives. But, Psalm 34:7 declares, *"For the angel of the LORD is a guard; he surrounds and defends all who fear him."*

God effected a great escape for Sarah according to Genesis 20:3-5 (NLT): *"But that night God came to Abimelech in a dream and told him, "You are a dead man, for that woman you have taken is already married!"* In his dream, Abimelech responded to God by advancing his innocence. Abraham had said that she was his sister and this was confirmed by Sarah.

God gave a response in Genesis 20:6,7 which demonstrated His knowledge and control of the minute details on planet earth:

> *In the dream God responded, Yes, I know you are innocent. That's why I kept you from sinning against me, and why I did not let you touch her. Now return the woman to her husband, and he will pray for you, for he is a prophet. Then you will live. But if you don't return her to him, you can be sure that you and all your people will die.*

Abimelech promptly returned Sarah to Abraham with rich presents to appease Abraham for the discomfort and embarrassment he had suffered. Moreover, he invited Abraham to choose an area that suited him for his dwelling place.

God Effected Lot's Great Escapes from Sodom

Sodom, where Lot and his family resided, was a wicked city. God made plans to destroy the entire population except for Lot and his family. God sent two angels to evacuate Lot and to destroy the city. Lot, who practiced hospitality according to Eastern tradition, saw the two strangers and invited them into his home. Genesis 19:4-7 (NLT) provides some details of what transpired:

> But before they retired for the night, all the men of Sodom young and old, came from all over the city and surrounded the house. They shouted to Lot, "Where are the men who came to spend the night with you? Bring them out to us so we can have sex with them!" So Lot stepped outside to talk to them, shutting the door behind him. "Please my brothers," he begged, "don't do such a wicked thing. Look, I have two virgin daughters. Let me bring them out to you, and you can do with them as you wish. But please, leave these men alone, for they are my guests and are under my protection." The men of Sodom were not aware that Lot's guests were angels sent to destroy the entire city. The angels pulled Lot inside of the house and struck the wicked men with blindness. The blindness convinced them to relent and return to their homes.

The angels urged Lot to gather his other children who lived in the city and get out of there to avoid destruction. However, those children and their spouses who lived outside of Lot's home ignored Lot's warning. The urgency of the situation was captured in Genesis 19:15-17 (NLT):

> At dawn the next morning the angels became insistent. "Hurry," they said to Lot. "Take your wife and your two daughters who are here. Get out right now, or you will be swept away in the destruction of the city!" When Lot still hesitated, the angels seized his hand and the hands of his wife and two daughters and rushed them to safety outside the city, for the LORD was merciful. When they were safely out of the city, one of the angels

ordered, "Run for your lives! And don't look back or stop anywhere in the valley! Escape to the mountains, or you will be swept away!"

Indeed, it was a great escape for Lot and his two daughters. Unfortunately, his wife disobeyed the instructions and looked back. As a result, she became a pillar of salt.

God Delivered Joseph Many Times

In Genesis chapters 39-41, the Scriptures relate how Joseph, the son of Jacob, found himself in situations where he experienced escape several times. His first escape was from a pit into which his brothers had thrown him and left him there to die. Later, they changed their minds, pulled him out of the pit and sold him as a slave.

While serving as a slave in Potiphar's household, Joseph ran away and escaped the sexual advances of Potiphar's wife. However, she lied on Joseph, claiming that Joseph tried to rape her. Joseph was thrown in jail for several years. When Joseph successfully interpreted Pharaoh's dream, he escaped from the prison sentence and was promoted to become the second in command in Egypt. It was God Who planned for Joseph to be in Egypt to help his father and brothers escape the famine that engulfed the entire area.

God Helped Esther And Her People Escape Destruction

King Xerxes, ruler of the Medes and Persians, had thrown a big party and gave instructions for his wife, Queen Vashti, to attend. Queen Vashti refused the invitation. The King and his advisors were embarrassed by Queen Vashti's attitude and decided to depose her and search for another queen. Esther became the new queen, but was instructed by her step father, Mordecai, to refrain from disclosing her Jewish lineage.

Haman, who had been promoted by the King, became furious because Mordecai refused to bow down to him. He learned that Mordecai was Jewish and soon devised a plan to destroy all the Jews. Haman even built a gallows on which Mordecai was to be hanged.

When Esther learned of Haman's threat to destroy all the Jews, she requested an audience with the King and informed him of Haman's plans. The King instructed that the Jews not only should be saved, but be given the power to destroy all their enemies. This was indeed a great escape for all the Jewish families of the kingdom.

The Great Escape From Sin

The greatest escape a human being could ever experience is the deliverance from sin. 1 Peter 4:18 supports this fact by stating, *"And if the righteous scarcely be saved, where shall the ungodly and the sinner appear?"* To understand the profound act of salvation, let us examine the Biblical descriptions of the human state prior to being saved. Ephesians 2:1-3 describes our state prior to our salvation:

> *Once you were dead because of your disobedience and your many sins. You used to live in sin, just like the rest of the world, obeying the devil—the commander of the powers in the unseen world. He is the spirit at work in the hearts of those who refuse to obey God. All of us used to live that way, following the passionate desires and inclinations of our sinful nature. By our very nature we were subject to God's anger, just like everyone else.*

God looked at our deplorable state and exercised His mercy and grace according to Ephesians 2:4-6 (NLT): *"But God is so rich in mercy, and he loved us so much, that even though we were dead because of our sins, he gave us life when he raised Christ from the dead. (It is only by God's grace that you have been saved!)"*

1 Corinthians 10:13 declares some additional help from God to ensure that we escape sin: *"There hath no temptation taken you but such as is common to man: but God is faithful, who will not suffer you to be tempted above that you are able; but will with the temptation also make a way to escape, that ye may be able to bear it."*

Colossians 1:19-22 (NLT) provide some more information about God's involvement in the believer's great escape from sin and the wrath of God:

> *For God in all his fullness was pleased to live in Christ, and through him God reconciled everything to himself. He made peace with everything in heaven and on earth by means of Christ's blood on the cross. This includes you who were once far away from God. You were his enemies, separated from him by your evil thoughts and actions. Yet now he has reconciled you to himself through the death of Christ in his physical body. As a result, he*

has brought you into his own presence, and you are holy and blameless as you stand before him without a single fault.

Wow! To be dead in trespasses and sin, subject to God's wrath, and the next moment to be considered by God to be without a single fault is certainly a great escape, especially since we could not and did not change ourselves.

I will submit that nobody in their right mind ought to neglect such a tremendous opportunity to escape God's wrath. Hebrews 2:3 declares:

How shall we escape, if we neglect so great salvation; which at the first began to be spoken by the Lord, and was confirmed unto us by them that heard him; God also bearing them witness, both with signs and wonders, and with divers miracles, and gifts of the Holy Ghost, according to his own will?

God's Promises To Provide Us With Escape

There are numerous divine promises given to us to encourage us regarding help for our escape. Why do we need to dwell on these promises? Remember the Word says in Psalm 91:4 (last part), *"His truth shall be thy shield and buckler."*

Our need for protection is also declared in Revelation 12:12: *"Therefore rejoice, ye heavens, and ye that dwell in them. Woe to the inhabiters of the earth and of the sea! For the devil is come down unto you, having great wrath, because he knoweth that he hath but a short time."* We certainly need help against the wrath of the enemy.

Concerning Divine help, Psalm 34:7 declares: *"The angel of the LORD encampeth round about them that fear him, and delivereth them."* In addition to what is above, Psalm 91:14,15 state: *"Because he hath set his love upon me, therefore will I deliver him: I will set him on high because he hath known my name. He shall call upon me, and I will answer him: I will be with him in trouble; I will deliver him, and honour him."*

Human beings constantly need deliverance from the traps set for us by the enemy. We need not be afraid. Let us praise and thank God that He has made us dwell in the secret place of the Most High so that we can always experience a great escape.

CHAPTER 13

Staying In God's Presence

There are two groups of people on planet earth, only two groups. You will meet them in Churches, you will meet them on the streets, you will meet them in the grocery, on school campuses and everywhere you go. The two groups are those who stay in God's presence and those who choose to walk away. Every human being begins life journey in God's presence, because through Jesus the world was reconciled back to God. However, many of us have allowed demonic guile and earthly distractions to separate us from God. In God's presence there is delightful joy, safety, fulfillment and complete satisfaction.

Remember, Adam and Eve began life's journey in God's presence but chose to walk away. The Israelites also began in God's presence for the Scriptures declared in 1 Corinthians 10:1-3 that they were all baptized and all drank of the spiritual drink. Unfortunately, many of them walked away from the Divine presence. This sermon is designed to encourage us to stay in God's presence.

The Benefits Of God's Presence

Human beings were created to live in and to enjoy God's presence. We could never be happy outside His embrace. Psalm 16:11 (NLT) declares: *"You will show me the way of life, granting me the joy of your presence and the pleasures of living with you forever."* Moreover, Jeremiah 17:7,8 describe the blessings that result from staying in God's presence:

> *But blessed are those who trust in the LORD and have made the LORD their hope and confidence. They are like trees planted along a riverbank, with roots that reach deep into the water. Such trees are not bothered by the heat or worried by long months of drought. Their leaves stay green, and they never stop producing fruit.*

The group that chose to walk away from God's presence because they are too busy to consistently seek God are described in Jeremiah 17:5,6 (NLT):

> This is what the LORD says: "Cursed are those who put their trust in mere humans, who rely on human strength and turn their hearts away from the LORD. They are like stunted shrubs in the desert, with no hope for the future. They will live in the barren wilderness, in an uninhabited salty land."

This passage of Scripture in Jeremiah 17:5-8 reminds me of the contrast between two areas of the African continent, the rain forest and the Sahara desert. The vast rain forest of Central Africa is teeming with an amazing variety of plant life and a huge variety of animals. Trees attain heights up to one hundred feet tall. The average rainfall is about one inch per day.

However, within that same continent, to the North of Africa is the location of the Sahara desert. It is a large area with no rainfall, lots of scorched, sandy dunes and few living things. The lack of rainfall and the scarcity of water produce a dry, arid land where few plants or animals survive. Note that although both areas are in Africa, the position or location of these two areas has been crucial in determining the amount of rainfall and the extent to which life can survive.

The contrast between the Sahara desert to the north of Africa and the rain forest located in the middle of the continent resembles the contrasting experiences of those who choose to remain positioned in God's presence and those who choose to exist outside of the Divine presence.

Isn't there an obvious difference between both groups? The ones that remain in the presence of the Lord and receive protection and sustenance from God are like green, fruitful trees. When heat and drought attack, these trees of righteousness are not concerned for they are positioned in the right place. Their roots have access to abundant water.

God has sent us literally hundreds of scriptures that encourage us to make the choice of getting back into His presence. Almost the whole of Psalm 91 deals with blessings of protection, deliverance and provision for those who choose to abide in His presence. Notice that the blessings are predicated on the condition of dwelling in God's presence according to Psalm 91:1,2: *"He that dwelleth in the secret place of the most High shall abide under the shadow of the Almighty. I will say of the LORD, He is my refuge and my fortress: my God; in him will I trust."*

Moreover, for those who dwell in His presence, Divine protection is offered according to Psalm 91:5-7, 10,11:

> *Thou shalt not be afraid for the terror by night; nor for the arrow that flieth by day; Nor for the pestilence that walketh in darkness; nor for the destruction that wasteth at noonday. A thousand shall fall at thy side, and ten thousand at thy right hand; but it shall not come nigh thee. There shall no evil befall thee, neither shall any plague come nigh thy dwelling. For he shall give his angels charge over thee, to keep thee in all thy ways.*

In addition to protection from harm and dangers, God's presence provides deliverance from trouble as described in Psalm 91:14,15: *"Because he hath set his love upon me, therefore will I will I deliver him: I will set him on high, because he hath known my name. He shall call upon me, and I will answer him: I will be with him in trouble; I will deliver him, and honour him."*

God Has Restored Everyone's Access To His Presence

When Adam and Eve sinned in the Garden, human beings made the choice to live apart from God's presence. However, the Divine mind anticipated the problem and made provisions for the prodigal sons and daughters, long before our birth according to 2 Timothy 1:9,10: *"Who hath saved us, and called us with an holy calling, not according to our works, but according to his own purpose and grace, which was given us in Christ Jesus before the world began,"*

Jesus ushered us back into God's presence according to 2 Corinthians 5:19: *"To wit, that God was in Christ, reconciling the world unto himself, not imputing their trespasses unto them; and hath committed unto us the word of reconciliation."*

Ephesians 2:4-6 supply us with more details about the reconciliation between God and man and our new positioning in Christ: *"But God, who is rich in mercy, for his great love wherewith he loved us, Even when we were dead in sins, hath quickened us together with Christ (by grace ye are saved;) And hath raised us up together, and made us sit together in heavenly places in Christ Jesus:"*

In addition to the above, we have the following instructions found in Colossians 3:2-4: *"Set your affection on things above, not on things on the earth. For ye are dead, and your life is hid with Christ in God. When Christ, who is our life, shall appear, then shall ye also appear with him in glory."*

God Demands Our Persistent, Passionate Response

Branches have no power of choice and automatically remain connected to trees. But human beings are intelligent and were created with the power of choice. Many distractions cause us to ignore God and despise His presence. We must make efforts to seek God fervently and passionately. In Jeremiah 29:13 God says to us: *"And ye shall seek me and, and find me, when ye shall search for me with all your heart."*

Halfhearted, lukewarm responses displease God. Notice how the members of the Laodicean Church were criticized for their lack of passion and enthusiasm in Revelation 3:14-16:

> *And unto the angel of the church of the Laodiceans write; These things saith the Amen, the faithful and true witness, the beginning of the creation of God; I know thy works, that thou art neither cold nor hot: I would thou wert cold or hot. So then because thou art lukewarm, and neither cold nor hot, I will spue thee out of my mouth.*

Additionally, in John 15:4,5 Jesus advised us: *"Abide in me, and I in you. As the branch cannot bear fruit of itself, except it abide in the vine; no more can ye except ye abide in me. I am the vine, ye are the branches: He that abideth in me, and I in him, the same bringeth forth much fruit: for without me ye can do nothing."*

How to Stay In God's Presence

Frequent meditating on God's Word and constant prayers are two methods of staying in His presence. Psalm 1:1,2 declares: *"Blessed is the man that walketh not in the counsel of the ungodly, nor standeth in the way of sinners, nor sitteth in the seat of the scornful. But his delight is in the law of the LORD; and in his law doth he meditate day and night."*

Note the blessings that follow those who frequently meditate on the Lord are described in Psalm 1:3: "And he shall be like a tree planted by the rivers of water, that bringeth forth his fruit in his season; his leaf also shall not wither; and whatsoever he doeth shall prosper."

In Joshua 1:8 we read: *"This book of the law shall not depart out of thy mouth; but thou shalt meditate therein day and night, that thou mayest observe to do according to all that is written therein: for then thou shalt make thy way prosperous, and then thou shalt have good success."*

Jesus spent a great deal of time meditating and praying to His Father. In Mark 1:35 we read: *"And in the morning, rising up a great while before day, he went out, and departed into a solitary place, and there prayed."*

John 14:10,11 implies that Jesus was consistently listening for instructions from His Father and allowing the Father to speak and work through him: *"Believest thou not that I am in the Father, and the Father in me? The words that I speak unto you I speak not of myself: but the Father that dwelleth in me, he doeth the works, Believe me that I am in the Father, and the Father in me: or else believe me for the very works sake."*

Some Persons In Bible Times Who Had Close Fellowship With God

An outstanding person in Bible times who spent a great deal of time in God's presence was Enoch. Genesis 5:22-24 (NLT) state: *"After the birth of Methuselah, Enoch lived in close fellowship with God for another 300 years, and he had other sons and daughters. Enoch lived 365 years, walking in close fellowship with God. Then one day he disappeared, because God took him."*

David was another person who spent much time in God's presence. Psalms 119:62 declares: *"At midnight I will rise to give thanks unto thee because of thy righteous judgments.* This tendency by David to frequently seek after God is supported in Psalm 55:17: *"Evening, and morning, and at noon, will I pray, and cry aloud: and he shall hear my voice."* We know that Daniel spent much time with God. Apart from his meditation, he got down on his knees and prayed three times a day as he was accustomed.

Note that Daniel continued the practice of seeking God's presence although there was a temporary law passed against petitioning someone else beside the King. Daniel 6:10 has the details: *"Now when Daniel knew that the writing was signed, he went into his house; and his windows being open in his chamber toward Jerusalem, he kneeled upon his knee three times a day, and prayed, and gave thanks before his God as he did aforetime."* King Darius of the Medes and Persians favored Daniel, but on the insistence of his accusers Daniel was thrown into a den of lions. However, God shut the lions' mouth and no harm came to him.

In the Book of Acts we are informed that the Early Church spent a great deal of time in God's presence according to Acts 2:46,47: *"And they, continuing daily with one accord in the temple, and breaking bread from house to house, did eat their meat with gladness and singleness of heart, Praising God, and having favour with all the people. And the Lord added to the church daily such as should be saved."*

In conclusion, when human beings, through persistent effort, take time to abide in God's presence, words are inadequate to describe the benefits. Throughout the Old and New Testaments God has been patiently, repetitiously inviting us to get into His presence. For the most part we have not taken God's words seriously. We become so engrossed in our own interests that seeking God's presence is placed on the back burner. Let us remember that in God's presence is fullness of joy and at His right hand there are pleasures for evermore.

CHAPTER 14

Nothing at All Could Go Wrong

Perhaps the most relevant Scripture that expresses the message that nothing at all could go wrong is found in Romans 8:28-32 (NLT) :

> *And we know that God causes everything to work together for the good of those who love God and are called according to his purpose for them. For God knew his people in advance, and he chose them to become like his Son, so that his Son would be the first born among many brothers and sisters. And having chosen them, he called them to come to him. And having called them, he gave them right standing with himself. And having given them right standing, he gave them his glory.*

We Are Always Winners

In this Scripture God declares that nothing in our lives would go wrong if we love Him. He will cause every incident and every situation in our lives to work together for our good. Regardless of what happens to us, God has already predestined that we come out of it as winners. This is indeed a fabulous Divine gift.

Secondly, did you notice in the Scripture previously cited state that God gave us right standing with Himself? What an awesome gift that the great God of Heaven and earth is satisfied with us and glorifies us! We all crave acceptance from other human beings. The extent to which we have been accepted by God is expressed in Romans 8:33: *"Who dares accuse us whom God has chosen for his own? No one–for God himself has given us right standing with himself."* There ought to be no room in our lives for low self-esteem or depression. We are so special in God's sight that He is displeased with anyone who criticizes us. This truth is found in Isaiah 54:17:

No weapon that is formed against thee shall prosper; and every tongue that shall rise against thee in judgment thou shalt condemn. This is the heritage of the servants of the LORD, and their righteousness is of me, saith the LORD.

All Things Worked Out Well For Joseph

Joseph must have wondered whether God had forgotten him. His brothers hated him because they were jealous that his father loved him and favored him. The Bible stated that his father had made him a coat of many colors. One day when the father sent Joseph to visit his brothers in the fields where they were taking care of the sheep, they took him and sold him as a slave. Joseph found himself isolated from his family and working as a slave in Egypt. Things got even worse when his master's wife falsely accused him of attempting to rape her. He was imprisoned for a crime he did not commit. In fact, it was his master's wife who had approached him and he ran away from her. But God had a plan for Joseph according to Psalm 105:17-21:

He sent a man before them, even Joseph, who was sold for a servant: whose feet they hurt with fetters: he was laid in iron: Until the time that his word came: the word of the LORD tried him. The king sent and loosed him; even the ruler of the people, and let him go free. He made him lord of his house, and ruler of all his substance:

When a deadly famine hit Egypt, Joseph was the one given wisdom by God to prepare Egypt by storing up food for seven years. God had allowed Joseph to be placed there in Egypt to preserve his father and the entire family. When his brothers came to purchase food in Egypt, Joseph recognized them, told them who he was and sent for the family to reside in Egypt.

Many times we fail to understand what God is doing behind the scenes. We fret and grumble when things seem to be going badly. Always remember that God is in control of all the circumstances and he has a plan for you. Remember, "All things work together for good to them that love God." You may not understand what is going on, but you must trust God and wait on Him. Isaiah 40:31 states, *"But they that wait upon the LORD shall renew their strength; they shall mount up with wings as eagles; they shall run, and not be weary; and they shall walk and not faint."*

David and Bathsheba

God is so merciful that even when we make mistakes He changes our mistakes into good. David, King of Israel, saw Uriah's wife and liked her. Uriah was a soldier who was away fighting the enemies of David. In Uriah's absence David got Uriah's wife, Bathsheba, pregnant. In addition to his sin of adultery, David arranged to have Uriah killed. God was very displeased with David, who took Bathsheba as his wife. That first baby, who came as a result of the union of David and Bathsheba died.

God had sent a prophet to tell David of his sin and David repented. 2 Samuel 12:9 provides information about God's displeasure with David: *"Wherefore hast thou despised the commandment of the LORD, to do evil in his sight? Thou hast killed Uriah the Hittite with the sword, and hast taken his wife to be thy wife, and hast slain him with the sword of the children of Ammon."*

It is amazing that God forgave David to such an extent that Jesus was born out of the lineage of David and Bathsheba. Although David had other wives, God chose Bathsheba to be the ancestor of Jesus to display His grace and His forgiveness.

We Must Avoid Speaking Evil of Others

It is a fact that people who speak evil of us will be condemned. However, God is also displeased when we "bad mouth or bad talk" others. Did you know that the Holy Angels are not allowed to speak evil of Satan? This is brought out in Jude 9: *But even Michael, one of the mightiest of the angels, did not dare accuse the devil of blasphemy, but simply said, "The Lord rebuke you!" (This took place when Michael was arguing with the devil about Moses' body.)"*

Additionally, we have been warned in Titus 3:2, *"To speak evil of no man, to be no brawlers, but gentle, shewing all meekness unto all men."*

We Must Never Fear

Based on these Divine promises we should never be afraid. A very frequent command that God gives us in His Word is to have no fear. In Luke 12:7 (NLT) God says to us, *"And the very hairs of on your head are all numbered. So don't be afraid; you are more valuable to God than a whole flock of sparrows."*

Dr. Grell Ferdinand

If we are so valuable to God that he knows the number of hairs on our heads, isn't He concerned and in control of every situation in our lives? God's concern for us and His control of every circumstance is revealed in Mark 4:37-41 (NLT) where an incident took place with Jesus and His disciples while they were in a boat crossing a lake:

> *But soon a fierce storm came up. High waves were breaking into the boat, and it began to fill with water. Jesus was sleeping at the back of the boat with his head on a cushion. The disciples woke him up, shouting, "Teacher, don't you care that we're going to drown?" When Jesus woke up, he rebuked the wind and said to the waves, "Silence! Be still!" Suddenly the wind stopped, and there was a great calm. Then he asked them, "Why are you afraid? Do you still have no faith?" The disciples were absolutely terrified. "Who is this man?" they asked each other. "Even the wind and waves obey him!"*

That same Jesus Who saved His disciples from drowning during the storm at sea, is still alive today and in control of all of our circumstances. He commands us to stop being afraid. Moreover, let us not forget that we are always in a win-win situation because we love the Lord. Recall that the Word says, *"And we know that all things work together for good to them that love the Lord."*

CHAPTER 15

Just Like a Baby

This sermon originated from the first song on my first CD, entitled, *Just Like A Baby*. There are several characteristics about little children that adults must learn and practice in order to become the persons that God wants us to be. Among the characteristics that God requires from us are humility, a willingness to be taught by others, the tendency to forgive and forget and dependence on God.

Humility

We recall that Jesus, the Creator of the universe, left the splendor of heaven and subjected Himself to a humble birth in a stable. In Philippians 2:5-8 we learn about the humility of Jesus which we must emulate in order to inherit the kingdom:

> *Let this mind be in you, which was also in Christ Jesus: Who, being in the form of God, thought it not robbery to be equal with God: But made himself of no reputation, and took upon himself the form of a servant, and was made in the likeness of men: And being found in fashion as a man, he humbled himself, and became obedient unto death, even the death of the cross.*

In Matthew 18:3,4 Jesus taught the importance of being as humble as a little child: *"And said, Verily I say unto you, Except ye be converted, and become as little children, ye shall not enter into the kingdom of heaven. Whosoever therefore shall humble himself as this little child, the same is greatest in the kingdom of heaven."*

We also remember that the Savior demonstrated humility when He girded Himself with a towel and washed His disciples' feet according to

John 13:4,5: *"He riseth from supper, and laid aside his garments; and took a towel, and girded himself. After that he poured water into a bason, and began to wash his disciples' feet, and to wipe them with the towel wherewith he was girded."*

Pride, which is the opposite of humility, is a characteristic we ought to avoid according to Proverbs 16:18: *"Pride goeth before destruction, and a haughty spirit before a fall."*

Willingness To Be Taught

Children tend to ask lots of questions, because they recognize their ignorance and are willing to learn. Many of us are unwilling to demonstrate how much we do not know. One line of the song says, *Just like a baby there is so much I don't know.* In 2 Timothy 2:15 we read, *Study to shew thyself approved unto God, a workman that needeth not to be ashamed, rightly dividing the word of truth."*

The disciples, most of them unlearned fishermen, followed Jesus everywhere He went, imbibing His teachings, His wisdom, His mannerisms and His power. Acts 4:13 declares that the leading religious leaders noticed a difference in the disciples of Jesus: *"Now when they saw the boldness of Peter and John, and perceiving that they were unlearned and ignorant men, they marveled; and they took knowledge of them that they had been with Jesus."*

The more time we spend in the presence of Jesus and with His word, the more we begin to resemble Him according to 2 Corinthians 3:18: *"But we all, with open face beholding as in a glass the glory of the Lord, are changed into the same image from glory to glory, even as by the Spirit of the Lord."*

The Tendency To Forgive And Forget

One notable characteristic of little children is their tendency to forgive and forget. A parent would punish a child and a short time after, the child would continue to show affection for the parent.

Whenever we are wronged, our philosophy ought to be like that of Jesus concerning those who crucified Him, *"Father forgive them for they know not what they have done."* Jesus also taught us in Luke 6:37: *"Judge not, and ye shall not be judged: condemn not, and ye shall not be condemned: forgive, and ye shall be forgiven."*

Depending Just Like A Baby

One of the most vulnerable of all creatures is a little baby, who depends on the caregiver for almost everything. That type of dependence must describe our relationship with our Heavenly Father. Dependence on God is perhaps the most valuable lesson we must learn from the song. The greatest mistake human beings can make is a lack of dependence on God. Jesus did nothing on His own.

As our human example, Jesus taught and demonstrated the principle of depending on God to do everything for Him. In John 5:30 (Amplified) Jesus declared:

> *I am able to do nothing from Myself [independently, of My own accord—but only as I am Taught by God and as I get his orders]. Even as I hear, I judge [I decide as I am bidden to Decide. As the voice comes to Me, so I give a decision], and My judgment is right (just, righteous) because I do not seek or consult My own will [I have no desire to do what is pleasing to Myself, My own aim, My own purpose] but only the will and pleasure of the Father Who sent Me."*

Obviously, this truth of total dependence on God contradicts the erroneous concept (held by many) that *"God helps those who help themselves."*

In John 14:10-12 the importance of allowing God to work through us is again taught by Jesus in the following words:

> *Believest not that I am in the Father, and the Father in me? The words that I speak unto you I speak not of myself: but the Father that dwelleth in me, he doeth the works. Believe me that I am in the Father, and the Father in me: or else believe me for the very works sake. Verily, verily, I say unto you, He that believeth in me, the works that I do shall he do also; and greater works than these shall he do; because I go unto my Father.*

Solomon's Prayer Of Dependence

God was so pleased with Solomon's prayer of dependence that he was given much more than he requested. 1 Kings 3:7-9 provide some details of Solomon's prayer:

And now O LORD my God, thou hast made thy servant king instead of David my father: and I am but a little child: I know not how to go out or come in. Give therefore thy servant an understanding heart to judge thy people, that I may discern between good and bad: for who is able to judge this thy so great a people?

Solomon told God that he was like a little child and needed all the help he could get. God was so pleased with Solomon's dependence that the Lord gave him more blessings than he asked for. The details of God's generous response is found in 1 Kings 3:12,13:

Behold, I have done according to thy words: lo, I have given thee a wise and understanding heart; so that there was none like thee before thee, neither after thee shall any arise like unto thee. And I have also given thee that which thou hast not asked, both riches and honour: so that there shall not be any among the kings like unto thee all thy days.

The Jewish Religious Leaders Failed To Depend

Romans 10:1-4 NLT) reveal that the Jewish religious leaders during the time of Christ had failed to depend like a baby to obtain salvation:

Dear brothers and sisters, the longing of my heart and my prayer to God is for the people of Israel to be saved. I know what enthusiasm they have for God, but it is misdirected zeal. For they don't understand God's way of making people right with himself. Refusing to accept God's way, they cling to their own way of getting right with God by trying to keep the law. For Christ has already accomplished the purpose for which the law was given. As a result, all who believe in him are made right with God.

Like those Jewish religious enthusiasts, many of us are not satisfied with simple childlike faith. We want to do something to help earn our salvation. Childlike, simple faith provides the result which we are trying so hard to accomplish by good works.

Divine Promises For Those Who Depend

A favorite promise of mine is found in Psalm 62:5,6: *"My soul, wait thou only upon God; for my expectation is from him. He only is my rock and my salvation: he is my defense; I shall not be moved."*

Isaiah 41:10 also provides peace and security even during anxious moments: *"Fear thou not; for I am with thee: be not dismayed; for I am thy God: I will strengthen thee; yea, I will help thee; yea, I will uphold thee with the right hand of my righteousness."*

Guidance is also promised in Proverbs 3:6: *"In all thy ways acknowledge him, and he shall direct thy paths."*

In conclusion, for Divine success let us borrow the characteristics of humility, willingness to be taught by others, the tendency to forgive and forget and total dependence on our Heavenly Father. Remember, unless we become as a little child we shall not inherit the kingdom of heaven. Let us pray: "Our Father in Heaven, we come to thee as little children, totally dependent for everything." We end with the words of the chorus of the song:

> *Ev'ry day in so many ways on you, Lord, I depend*
> *Protecting me sustaining me, faithful to the end*
> *Just like a baby in Your likeness let me grow*
> *Fill me with Your Spirit and my joy will overflow.*

CHAPTER 16

These Signs Shall Follow
Them that Believe

Mark 16:17,18 declare, *"And these signs shall follow them that believe; In my name shall they cast out devils; they shall speak with new tongues; They shall take up serpents; and if they drink any deadly thing, it shall not hurt them; they shall lay hands on the sick, and they shall recover."*

God did not give us signs, wonders and miracles just to provide inspiration, amazement and awe. Signs, wonders and miracles are critical. There are at least three reasons why signs, wonders and miracles will continue to take place in this world until Jesus comes.

Firstly, we live on a planet occupied with evil, supernatural beings that hate us and frequently attack us. Ephesians 6:12 informs us that we wrestle not against flesh and blood but against principalities and powers. Since we cannot conquer these principalities in our own human strength, we need supernatural assistance.

Revelation 12:12 declares, *"Therefore rejoice, ye heavens, and ye that dwell in them. Woe to the inhabitants of the earth and of the sea! For the devil is come down unto you, having great wrath, because he knoweth that he hath but a short time."* These enemies, these unseen principalities and powers are angry. Hence it is time that the servants of God become filled with righteous indignation against these wicked foes and cast them out of our lives and the lives of our relatives and neighbors. It is high time that we get vex. Have you ever witnessed a hurricane or a tornado? Hurricanes and tornados seem to be angry.

The goal of this sermon is to stir us up to become angry at what the devil is doing. Generally, we have been accepting all his blows without complaints and without resistance. We are too complacent. We need to fight back.

Thirdly, we need signs, wonders and miracles because we live in a sinful, degenerate world with lots of human needs, some of which, can only be met with miraculous interventions. The Scripture never teaches that we are to supply our needs by ourselves.

In Philippians 4:19 we are told that our needs are to be supplied by supernatural means. Let us all repeat Philippians 4:19 together: *"But my God shall supply all your needs according to his riches in glory by Christ Jesus."* The Scripture states that God will do the supplying. Abraham understood that he needed God's help.

Abraham's Wife Delivered Miraculously

Abraham found himself with a problem that he could not solve on his own. Fortunately for him he trusted God. Abraham believed in miracles, that is why he is called the father of faith. While living in Gerar, although he lied and said to King Abimelech that Sarah was his sister, God delivered Sarah back to Abraham.

She had been taken by Abimelech to become one of his wives. This account is found in Genesis chapter 20. Let us look at Genesis 20:3,4,5 where God, Abraham's defender, speaks very sternly to Abimelech:

> *But God came to Abimelech in a dream by night, and said to him, Behold, thou art but a dead man, for the woman which thou hast taken; for she is a man's wife. But Abimelech had not come near her: and he said, Lord, wilt thou slay also a righteous nation?*
> *Said he not unto me, She is my sister? And she even she herself said He is my brother: in the integrity of my heart and innocency of my hands have I done this.*

God appeared unto Abimelech the second time and instructed him to restore Abraham's wife which he promptly did. In Genesis 20:14 we read, *"And Abimelech took sheep, and oxen, and menservants, and women servants, and gave them unto Abraham, and restored him Sarah his wife."*

What is also amazing is that God now instructs the same Abraham who had deceived Abimelech to pray for Abimelech and his people according to Genesis 20:17,18: *"So Abraham prayed unto God: and God healed Abimelech, and his wife, and his maidservants; and they bare children. For the LORD had fast closed up all the wombs of the house of Abimelech, because of Sarah Abraham's wife."*

Dr. Grell Ferdinand

David Experienced Lots of Miracles

Among the experiences that David had were the occasions when he killed a lion and a bear on different occasions. It was not with a gun or some modern equipment. It was like hand to hand combat with the help of a club according to 1 Samuel 17:3,4,35 (NLT version).

These experiences provided him with the confidence to tackle Goliath. In 1 Samuel 17:4,5,46,47 we find the account of the slaying of Goliath. It was God who really killed Goliath with David as an instrument in God's hands. In 1 Samuel 17:46, David tells Goliath, *"Today the LORD will conquer you, and I will kill you and cut off your head. And I will give the dead bodies of your men to the birds and wild animals, and the whole world will know that there is a God in Israel!"*

Job Experienced God's Miracles

Job got into problems that he certainly did not initiate. All his children were killed, his possessions were stolen and his body was not just afflicted with something simple, but with a horrible infirmity with sores and worms.

For Job to be healed took a miracle. Moreover, to recover from the loss of his possessions and to become twice as wealthy as he was before took another miracle from his God. In Job 42:10 we read, *"And the LORD turned the captivity of Job, when he prayed for his friends: and the LORD gave Job twice as much as he had before."*

God Worked Several Miracles For Daniel

We need to be convinced that we don't have to go looking for trouble. Instead trouble comes looking for us, and the problem is that most of them are bigger than we could handle. Psalm 34:19 declares, *"Many are the afflictions of the righteous: but the Lord delivereth him out of them all."* One day, Arioch, the captain of the king's guard, came to see Daniel.

I could imagine Daniel greeting him, "Good morning Mr. Arioch, what can I do for you?" Arioch responded, "I have come to kill you and your friends. Daniel responds, "Is this some kind of joke?" Arioch: "I wish it were, my friend, but this is the King's orders." He then explains to Daniel the dialogue that took place between some of the wise men in the kingdom and King Nebuchadnezzar.

We know the story how Daniel begged Arioch for time, then he went and told his Hebrew friends the problem they faced and, of course, asked them to pray for a miracle. In Daniel 2:19 we read, *"Then was the secret revealed unto Daniel in a night vision. Then Daniel blessed the God of heaven."*

When Daniel and his friends were in deep trouble, God showed up, revealing the dream and the interpretation to Daniel.

The King was so pleased that he promoted Daniel and his other friends. This was one of several experiences when God intervened in Daniel's life.

After that miraculous intervention by God, Daniel got into trouble again. On this occasion, King Nebuchadnezzar set up an image of gold relating to his false gods and commanded everyone to bow down to the image. Of course, Daniel's companions refused.

They were thrown into a fiery furnace. Daniel 3:24,25 relates the response of the King as he sees an extra person walking in the furnace with the three men that had been thrown in:

> *Then Nebuchadnezzar the king was astonished, and rose up in haste, and spake and said unto his counselors, Did not we cast three men bound into the midst of the fire? They answered unto the king, True, O king. He answered and said, Lo, I see four men loose, walking in the midst of the fire, and they have no hurt; and the form of the fourth is like the Son of God.*

As a result of this astonishing miracle, Nebuchadnezzar made a decree that only Daniel's God be recognized in the kingdom. Moreover, Daniel's friends were promoted to higher positions. Do the people of God need signs, wonders and miracles? Oh yes, the do.

We will not get into the details of the miraculous deliverance of Daniel from the hungry jaws of the lions. But suffice it to say that no one could have convinced Daniel and his companions that signs, wonders and miracles were not essential for human survival.

Jesus, the Miracle Worker

Everyone is acquainted with the miraculous works of Jesus. His very birth was a miracle. We recall how Joseph was baffled at the pregnancy of Mary and had planned to put her away privately.

However, an angel appeared unto him in a dream by night and explained that Mary's conception was by the Holy Ghost. This account is found in Matthew 1:20,21. We recall at his baptism the Holy Ghost alighted on Jesus in the form of a dove and a voice from heaven identified Jesus as God's Beloved Son.

All the miracles performed by Jesus are too numerous for us to detail. However, we remember that he turned water into wine, fed five thousand men beside women and children with five loaves and two fishes, commanded the storm to be still when it threatened the lives of His disciples.

Are miracles important today? Jesus proved that they are essential. Acts 10:38 declares, *"How God anointed Jesus of Nazareth with the Holy Ghost and with power: who went about doing good, and healing all that were oppressed with of the devil: for God was with him."*

Note that the storm attacking the boat with the disciples of Jesus was an angry display by the devil. How did Jesus respond to the Satanic outburst? "Shut up and allow peace to reign." Were miracles necessary during the life of Jesus on earth? Of course they were. The people had needs that could only be satisfied by miraculous, supernatural, Heavenly interventions. And Jesus responded to their needs.

The Scriptues said that Jesus went about doing good and healing not some but all that were oppressed by the devil. Is the devil still oppressing people today? What are we doing about the current diabolic oppression?

We recall the Apostle Paul telling Timothy in 2 Timothy 1:6,7,9:

> *Wherefore I put thee in remembrance that thou stir up the gift of God, which is in thee by the putting on of my hands. For God hath not given us the spirit of fear; but of power, and of love, and of a sound mind. Who hath saved us, and called us with an holy calling, not according to our works, but according to his own purpose and grace.*

The Scripture reminds us to stir up the gifts that are in all of us; that we should not be afraid of the devil and his angry outbursts; that God has given us His love. This love will motivate us to have compassion on those around us who are being oppressed by the devil; also God has given us power. He said in Luke 10:19: *"Behold, I give unto you power to tread on serpents and scorpions, and over all the power of the enemy: and nothing shall by any means hurt you."*

CHAPTER 17

When Things Seem Impossible

"Ah Lord God! Behold, Thou hast made the heaven and the earth by thy great power and stretched out arm, and there is nothing too hard for thee." (Jeremiah 32:17).

Ever so often every one of us faces threats and challenges that seem too hard or even impossible to overcome. Whenever we encounter these tests of faith, let us be aware that our situation is not abnormal. Situations that seem impossible to overcome are experienced by everyone, young and old, rich and poor, the righteous and the unrighteous. Every outstanding child of God recorded in the Bible faced circumstances that seemed impossible to overcome. Abraham and Sarah, the Israelites, Elisha, David, Paul, Silas and Jesus, to name a few, found themselves facing situations that seemed humanly impossible.

Know the Source of Your Help

Since we all will face uncommon difficulties that seem impossible, therefore, everyone both Christians and non-Christians should be given a thorough education concerning how to deal with circumstances that seem impossible to overcome. Psalm 121:1,2 (NLT) should be a part of that education. This Scripture teaches us where to fix our eyes when troubles come: *"I look up to the mountains—does my help come from there? My help comes from the LORD, who made heaven and earth."*

Another aspect of our education is recorded in Psalm 46:1,2: *"God is our refuge and strength, always ready to help in times of trouble. So we will not fear when earthquakes come and the mountains crumble into the sea."* Every man, woman and child in Haiti should have been thoroughly grounded in this Scripture, considering the damage done by the disastrous earthquake.

Even righteous people suffer from afflictions. But note that they will be delivered according to Psalm 34:19 (NLT): *"The righteous person faces many troubles, but the LORD comes to the rescue each time."*

Psalm 91:15 ought to be included in this education. It declares: *"He shall call upon me, and I will answer him: I will be with him in trouble; I will deliver him, and honour him."*

Our education must also include Isaiah 41:10 where God reminds us: *"Fear thou not; for I am with thee: be not dismayed; for I am thy God: I will strengthen thee; yea, I will help thee; yea, I will uphold thee with the right hand of my righteousness."*

Therefore, although we face situations and circumstances that may seem impossible, we ought to expect miracles of deliverance every time. The following miraculous deliverances are recorded to teach us how to respond when things seem impossible.

Ninety Year Old Woman Gives Birth To A Baby

Abraham and Sarah had a problem. In the Eastern custom, it was a disgrace to be married and childless. In fact, according to their tradition, to go childless was to be under a curse. Although Abraham and Sarah were financially successful, people placed them in a lower social category because they had not been blessed with children. Both Abraham and Sarah had far exceeded child-bearing age.

But God saw their dilemma and made plans to fix it. Several times they had been reminded that God would bless them with an entire generation produced from their own bodies. When the time came, God fulfilled His promise. Here are the details in Genesis 21:1,2,3:

> *And the LORD visited Sarah as he had said, and the LORD did unto Sarah as he had spoken. For Sarah conceived, and bare Abraham a son in his old age, at the set time of which God had spoken to him. And Abraham called the name of his son that was born unto him, whom Sarah bare to him, Isaac.*

When things seem impossible, understand that God has a plan. Never give up. Remember, God loves to show His power when things seem impossible as happened to the Israelites.

More than 600,000 People Cross the Sea Without Boats

No airplanes, no submarines, no helicopters and no boats were employed in this operation. Yet more than 600,000 crossed over safely from one shore of the Red Sea across to the other distant shore. The account of this historic miracle is found in Exodus Chapter 14. Here are the details in Exodus 14: 21-23 of how the sea water parted, piled up on both sides of a dry strip of land, wide enough for the Israelites to cross over:

> *And Moses stretched out his hand over the sea; and the LORD caused the sea to go back by a strong east wind all that night, and made the sea dry land, and the waters were divided. And the children of Israel went into the midst of the sea upon the dry ground: and the waters were a wall unto them on their right hand, and on their left.*

What a marvelous sight that must have been! Wouldn't you, Dear reader, have been thrilled to witness God's power in action? There were two high walls of water on both sides with a wide strip of dry land between. Mothers with their babies being held protectingly, old men and women together with the stronger, younger ones all hurrying across to the other side.

They were alert and they were hurrying because according to Exodus 14:23 the Egyptian army was pursuing them: *"And the Egyptians pursued, and went in after them to the midst of the sea, even all Pharaoh's horses, his chariots, and his horsemen."*

The pursuit went on all night. However, by the next day as the Israelites crossed over safely to the other side of the Red Sea, God gave Moses some more instructions that destroyed the threat to the Israelites. Exodus 14:26,27 provide the details:

> *And the LORD said unto Moses, Stretch out thine hand over the sea, that the waters may come again upon the Egyptians, upon their chariots, and upon their horsemen. And Moses stretched forth his hand over the sea, and the sea returned to his strength when the morning appeared; and the Egyptians fled against it; and the LORD overthrew the Egyptians in the midst of the sea.*

All of us have enemies that threaten our existence. Let us allow our mighty Deliverer to destroy these enemies that pursue us. When things seem impossible, the Omnipotent One will step in to fight our enemies.

Dr. Grell Ferdinand

Two Dead Men Interact And One Comes Alive

This is also an astounding miracle. Elisha, a powerful prophet of God had died so long that only his bones remained. However, according to 2 Kings 13:20,21 the power of God would still produce a wonderful miracle:

> *And Elisha died, and they buried him. and the bands of the Moabites invaded the land at the coming of the year. And it came to pass, as they were buring a man, that, behold, they spied a band of men; and they cast the man into the sepulcher of Elisha: and when the man was let down, and touched the bones of Elisha, he revived, and stood up on his feet.*

Wow! What an astounding miracle. Two dead men interact and one helps to resurrect the other. The power of God was still in the bones of Elisha. God's power in Elisha's dead body produced a resurrection. Is there anything too hard for God? Obviously, the answer is no. Let us investigate another miracle.

David Experienced Several Threats and Challenges

David saw the power of God working miraculous deliverances on his behalf on many occasions. In his effort to convince King Saul that he qualified to confront Goliath, the giant, David explained: *"David said moreover, The LORD that delivered me out of the paw of the lion, and out of the paw of the bear, he will deliver me out of the hand of this Philistine. And Saul said unto David, Go, and the LORD be with thee."* We are aware that God used David to kill Goliath and bring victory to the Israelites.

After David became king, his son, Absalom, made plans to wrench the throne from his father. Absalom established himself in Hebron and prepared for war against his father, David.

David was forced to leave his home. Things did seem impossible because Absalom had over a period of several years craftily gained the admiration and confidence of many people in Israel. Both groups, Absalom's army and David' army began to fight. God did not abandon David. According to 2 Samuel 18:9,15 Absalom was killed:

> *And Absalom met the servants of David. And Absalom rode upon a mule, and the mule went under the thick boughs of a great oak, and his head*

caught hold of the oak, and he was taken up between the heaven and the earth; and the mule that was under him went away. And ten young men that bare Joab's armour compassed about and smote Absalom, and slew him.

Once more when things seemed impossible, God came to the rescue.

God Delivers Paul and Silas

Things did seem impossible for Paul and Silas. They did nothing wrong. They were simply preaching the gospel. However, the enemies of Christ caused them to be imprisoned. Here are some of the details in Acts 16:23-26:

And when they had laid many stripes upon them, they cast them into prison, charging the jailor to keep them safely: who, having received such a charge, thrust them into the inner prison, and made their feet fast in the stocks. And at midnight Paul and Silas prayed, and sang praises unto God: and the prisoners heard them. And suddenly there was a great earthquake, so that the foundations of the prison were shaken: and immediately all the doors were opened, and every one's bands were loosed.

Note all the precautions that were taken to ensure that they would not escape. They were placed in the inner prison. Their feet were shackled with iron chains. But an amazing thing happened. God sent an earthquake. Apparently, there are good earthquakes and bad earthquakes. There are those that cause destruction like as in Haiti. Then there are the earthquakes that loose chains from prisoners. Nothing is impossible with God.

As a result of this incident the jailor and his entire family got saved.

Man comes Alive 4 Days After Buriel

Jesus was far away from Mary, Martha and Lazarus when Lazarus took sick. John 11:3 give us the details of the response of Jesus when he got the news: *"Therefore his sisters sent unto him, saying, Lord, behold, he whom thou lovest is sick. When Jesus heard that, he said, this sickness is not unto death, but for the glory of God, that the Son of God might be glorified thereof."*

Jesus knew of the impending death of Lazarus, and had plans to raise him to life again, but did not disclose his plans to anyone. In fact, he

Dr. Grell Ferdinand

seemed to have ignored the sorrowful plight of the sisters for in John 11:6 we are told, *"When he had heard therefore that he was sick, he abode two days still in the same place where he was."*

Did Jesus care? Of course He cared. He already knew what He would do. Similarly, when we implore for some need to be fulfilled, we seem not to get a response from God. However, He said in Isaiah 65:24, *"And it shall come to pass, that before they call, I will answer; and while they are yet speaking, I will hear."*

John 11:43,44 provides information about the remarkable resurrection of Lazarus: *"And when he thus had spoken, he cried with a loud voice, Lazarus, come forth. And he that was dead came forth, bound hand and foot with graveclothes: and his face was bound about with a napkin. Jesus saith unto them, Loose him and let him go."*

Jeremiah 32:27 declares, *"Behold, I am the LORD, the God of all flesh: is anything too hard for me?* Moreover, we are told in Psalm 91 that no evil will befall us and that when we call upon the Lord in our trouble, He will answer us. In Psalm 46:1 we are reminded that God is our refuge and strength, a very present help in trouble.

Therefore, when things seem impossible, let us remember that nothing is impossible with God. We must trust and not be afraid.

CHAPTER 18

If God Says So It Is So

Whatever God says exists. The same moment that the Divine word is uttered it becomes a reality. Biblical records attest to the fact that God's word never fails. The time has come for God's children to believe His promises because whatever He says is true and must always happen. While blessings belong to those who believe and act on God's word, destruction follow the unbeliever.

The truthfulness and the power of God's Word is expressed in Psalm 33:9 which states, *"For he spake, and it was done, He commanded and it stood fast."* The following Scripture found in Numbers 23:19 (NLT) supports this truth about the veracity of God's word: *"God is not a man so He does not lie. He is not human, so He does not change His mind. Has He ever spoken and failed to act? Has He ever promised and not carried it through?"*

Here is another Scripture found in Isaiah 55:10,11 (NLT) that describes the truth of God's word:

> *The rain and snow come down from the heavens and stay on the ground to water the earth. They cause the grain to grow, producing seed for the farmer and bread for the hungry. It is the same with my word. I send it out, and it always produces fruit. It will accomplish all I want it to, and it will prosper everywhere I send it.*

The Psalmist David recognized the faithfulness of God's promises and expressed his awe and gratitude in these words found in Psalm 138:2: *"I bow before your holy temple as I worship. I praise your name for your unfailing love and faithfulness; for your promises are backed by all the honor of your name."*

What God Promised Regarding Our Health

Since we are now convinced that our Omnipotent and loving Heavenly Father always fulfills His promises, let us now visit some Divine promises regarding our health. Psalm 103:2,3 declare: *"Bless the LORD, O my soul, and forget not all his benefits: Who forgiveth all thine iniquities; who healeth all thy diseases."* It is now our responsibility to repeat, believe and claim the perfect health God has promised us.

Isaiah 53:4,5 report the role of Jesus in providing good health to all of us: *"But he was wounded for our transgressions, he was bruised for our iniquities: the chastisement of our peace was upon him; and with his stripes we are healed."*

God's desire to heal us is also brought out in Acts 10:38 which tells about God's activities through His Son, Jesus: *"How God anointed Jesus of Nazareth with power: who went about doing good and healing all that were oppressed of the devil: for God was with him."*

There are numerous methods by which we can be healed. One method is declared in James 5:15-16:

> *Is anyone among you sick? Let him call for the elders of the church, and let them pray over him, anointing him with oil in the name of the Lord. And the prayer of faith will save the sick, and the Lord will raise him up. And if he has committed sins, he will be forgiven. Confess your trespasses one to another, and pray for one another, that you may be healed. The effectual fervent prayer of a righteous man availeth much.*

God's willingness to heal is also brought out in Matthew 8:16,17:

> *When the even was come, they brought unto him many that were possessed with devils: and he cast out the spirits with his word, and healed all that were sick: that it might be fulfilled which was spoken by Esaias the prophet, saying, HIMSELF TOOK OUR INFIRMITIES, AND BARE OUR SICKNESSES.*

Believers have been given a special mandate to heal the sick and cast out demons in Mark 16:17,18:

And these signs shall follow them that believe; In my name shall they cast out devils; they shall speak with new tongues; They shall take up serpents; and if they drink any deadly thing, it shall not hurt them; they shall lay hands on the sick, and they shall recover.

God's Promises Regarding Our Finances

We have a rich Heavenly Father Who promises to faithfully take care of the needs of His children. Psalm 23:1 (NLT) says, *"The LORD is my shepherd; I have all that I need."* In addition to the above, Psalm 37:18,19 declare: *"The LORD knoweth the days of the upright: and their inheritance shall be forever, They shall not be ashamed in the evil time: and in the days of famine they shall be satisfied."*

Let us remember that God cannot lie. And His word can't return to Him void. More assurances are given in Matthew 6:31, 33: *"Therefore take no thought, saying, What shall we eat? Or, What shall we drink? Or, wherewith shall we be clothed? But seek ye first the kingdom of God, and his righteousness; and all these things shall be added unto you."*

Here is another promise in Isaiah 45:3 which must not be neglected: *"And I will give thee the treasures of darkness, and hidden riches of secret places, that thou mayest know that I, the LORD, which call thee by thy name, am the God of Israel."*

God Who cannot lie, reveals another promise in Psalms 112:1-3 which will enrich those who love and respect Him:

Praise ye the LORD. Blessed is the man that feareth the LORD, that deligeth greatly in his commandments. His seed shall be mighty upon earth: the generation of the upright shall be blessed. Wealth and riches shall be in his house: and his righteousness endureth for ever.

What God Promised Regarding Your Children

God loves to take care of a whole group, including a person and their family. He does not limit His blessings to just one individual. In Isaiah 54:13 the Lord states: *"All your children shall be taught of the LORD, And great shall be the peace of your children."*

Additionally, in Isaiah 59:21 (NLT) God promises: *"And this is my covenant with them, says the LORD. My Spirit will not leave them, and neither will these words I have given you. They will be on your lips and on the lips of your children and your children's children forever. I, the LORD, have spoken it."*

We recall that not only Abraham was blessed, but so was Isaac and Jacob and their descendants. Also, Noah and his household were all saved from the raging flood waters. In the Book of Acts, the jailor was told, ". . . *Believe on the Lord Jesus Christ, and thou shalt be saved, and thy house."*

God's Promises For Us To Walk In Signs And Wonders

In order for us to become efficient workers for God we must walk in signs and wonders. Jesus told us in Luke 10:19, *"Behold, I give unto you power to tread on serpents and scorpions, and over all the power of the enemy: and nothing shall by any means hurt you."*

In addition, Jesus instructed all His followers to go and preach the gospel in all the world. He continued this mandate by saying in Mark 16:17,18: *"And these signs shall follow them that believe; In my name shall they cast out devils; they shall speak with new tongues; They shall take up serpents; and if they drink any deadly thing, it shall not hurt them; they shall lay hands on the sick, and they shall recover."*

The ministry performed by Jesus according to Isaiah 61:2,3 ought to be performed by His modern disciples:

> *To proclaim the acceptable year of the LORD, and the day of vengeance of our God; to comfort all that mourn; To appoint unto them that mourn in Zion, to give them beauty for ashes, the oil of joy for mourning, the garment of praise for the spirit of heaviness; that they might be called trees of righteousness, the planting of the LORD, that he might be glorified.*

There are lots of people around us who are groping in darkness. What does God say we ought to do? Isaiah 60:1-3 provides the information concerning Divine help for us to perform our responsibilities:

> *Arise, shine; for thy light is come, and the glory of the LORD is risen upon thee. For, behold, the darkness shall cover the earth, and gross darkness the people: but the LORD shall arise upon thee, and his glory shall be seen upon thee. And the Gentiles shall come to thy light, and kings to the brightness of thy rising.*

It is Dangerous to Despise God's Word

Although so many blessings are attached to those who respect and carry out God's word, on the other hand Biblical records attest to the fact that it is dangerous to despise or ignore His instructions.

God had instructed Adam to eat of every tree of the Garden except from the tree of knowledge of good and evil. The consequences of despising God's words were clearly spelled out according to Genesis 2:16,17: *"And the LORD God commanded the man, saying, Of every tree of the garden thou mayest freely eat: But of the tree of the knowledge of good and evil, thou shalt not eat of it: for in the day that thou eatest thereof thou shalt surely die."*

Satan told Adam and Eve that they may eat of the forbidden fruit without suffering death. In other words, Satan implied that God's word should be ignored. The entire human race suffered the consequences of despising God's word. 1 Corinthians 5:22 declares, *"For as in Adam all die, even so in Christ shall all be made alive."* Thank God that we were all raised up at the resurrection of Jesus according to Colossians 2:13 (NLT): *"You were dead because of your sins and because your sinful nature was not yet cut away. Then God made you alive with Christ, for he forgave all our sins."*

Further support regarding our death and resurrection is found in Ephesians 2:6 (NLT): *"For he raised us from the dead along with Christ and seated us with him in the heavenly realms because we are united with Christ Jesus."*

In 2 Kings chapter 6 we find the record of the consequences of failure to respect God's word. There was a great famine in the land of Samaria. The King of Syria had gathered an army and surrounded the city of Samaria. Food became so scarce that two women agreed to kill and cook their two sons in order for them to survive.

However, God had planned to provide relief and sent the following message through Elisha: *"Then Elisha said, Hear ye the word of the LORD; Thus saith the LORD, To morrow about this time shall a measure of fine flour be sold for a shekel, and two measures of barley for a shekel, in the gate of Samaria."*

A top official, who was in close fellowship with the King of Samaria despised God's word according to 2 Kings 7:2: *"Then a lord on whose hand the king leaned answered the man of God, and said, Behold, if the LORD would make windows in heaven, might this thing be? And he said, Behold, thou shalt see it with thine eyes, but shall not eat thereof."*

Dr. Grell Ferdinand

Four lepers of Samaria had made a decision to venture into the camp of the Syrians in search of food. They discovered that the entire Syrian army had vanished. God had caused the Syrians to hear sounds that made them feel that a larger army than theirs was coming to attack them. The men of the Syrian army took off running and left all their food and their valuables behind.

The lepers who discovered that the enemies had disappeared soon spread the word and the people of Samaria began to rush out through the city gate to obtain food and valuables. Meanwhile the king had ordered the skeptical official on whose hand he had leaned, to organize the people and control the traffic through the gate. The people, in their haste to obtain food, trampled the official and he died. Indeed it is dangerous to disregard or despise God's word.

In conclusion, let us believe and claim God's promises. Moreover, let us rise up and shine for He has promised that He will shine through us to bring light to a world in darkness. If God said so, it is so.

CHAPTER 19

Divine Favor

Favor is defined by Webster's Dictionary as *"an act of generosity; privilege granted; the state or condition of being favored or approved."* In addition to these, I want to add as my own definition that favor means preferential treatment. Although God's grace, which includes preferential treatment, is freely given to everyone, Biblical records show that there are several persons in the Bible who received outstanding preferential treatment from God. Among them were Abraham, David, Joseph, Esther, Mary, the mother of Jesus, and many others.

In most cases preferential treatment is not something that is earned. It is, in fact, given to someone who is favored and comes rather spontaneously. However, God has laid out certain conditions by which every human being can enjoy Divine favor. Every time I read Deuteronomy, chapter twenty-eight, I am fascinated by the variety of blessings and favor that God offers those who fulfill the conditions of obedience.

Concerning obedience to God and the resulting favor that can be received, here is a fitting illustration. Although the sun is always shining, there are portions of the earth that receive sunlight, while other parts remain in darkness. There are parts of the earth that are positioned to receive direct sunlight. Of course we understand that favorable positioning comes as a result of the earth's revolution around the sun. Similarly, when we obey God we make decisions to position ourselves to receive multiple blessings. It is amazing that God has such a span of control that He can bring us preferential treatment and blessings in all the a variety of ways described in Deuteronomy 28.

Deuteronomy 28:3,4 (NLT) states, *"Your towns and your fields will be blessed. Your children and your crops will be blessed."* There are four types of blessings mentioned in these two verses.

In Deuteronomy 28:5,6 (NLT) we read, "Your fruit baskets and breadboards will be blessed. Wherever you go and whatever you do, you will be blessed. Here are four more blessings promised. Moreover, note that *"wherever you go"* and *"whatever you do"* are expressions that cover a very wide span of blessings. Wouldn't you just love to be blessed in whatever you do and wherever you go?

Deuteronomy 28:7,8 declares: *"The LORD will conquer your enemies when they attack you. They will attack you from one direction, but they will scatter from you in seven! The LORD will guarantee a blessing on everything you do and will fill your storehouses with grain. The LORD your God will bless you in the land he is giving you."* Your enemies can be anything that attacks – whether it be human beings, illness or poverty. Filling your storehouses with grain was promised because the original people spoken to, lived in an agrarian society. However, to be relevant to ourselves we can think of successful bank accounts.

In Deuteronomy 28:9,10 we learn that God will establish us as His holy people and nations all over the world will recognize and be impressed that God's mighty power is caring for us: *"If you obey the commands of the LORD your God and walk in his ways, the LORD will establish you as his holy people as he swore he would do. Then all the nations of the world will see that you are a people claimed by the LORD, and they will stand in awe of you."*

Deuteronomy 28:11,12 (LNT) declare:

> The LORD will give you prosperity in the land he swore to your ancestors to give you, blessing you with many children, numerous livestock, and abundant crops. The LORD will send rain at the proper time from his rich treasury in the heavens and will bless all the work you do. You will lend to many nations, but you will never need to borrow from them.

Deuteronomy chapter 28 contains such a variety of blessings that God seemed determined to omit nothing good. However, never forget that these divine blessings were contingent on man's obedience.

Conditions For Divine Favor

The conditions that we must fulfill to receive the fabulous blessings of Deuteronomy 28 is declared in verse 1: *"Now it shall come to pass, if you diligently obey the voice of the LORD your God, to observe carefully all His commandments which I command you today, that the Lord your God will set you on high above all nations of the earth."*

This Scripture is stating that when we diligently obey God, we put ourselves in position for numerous favors. How can we diligently obey God?

It is important for us to pause here to declare that faith in Jesus allows us to appropriate His righteousness and thus be regarded as diligently obedient. This truth is described in Romans 5:18,19 (NLT): *"Yes, Adam's one sin brings condemnation for everyone, but Christ's one act of righteousness brings a right relationship with God and new life for everyone. Because one person disobeyed God, many became sinners. But because one other person obeyed God, many will be made righteous."*

Our faith in Jesus allows us to be considered by God as righteous or diligently obedient. We recall that Abraham believed God and he was considered to be righteous. This fact is found in Romans 4:2,3: *"For if Abraham were justified by works, he hath whereof to glory; but not before God. For what saith the Scripture? ABRAHAM BELIEVED GOD, AND IT WAS COUNTED UNTO HIM FOR RIGHTEOUSNESS."*

A very encouraging Scripture found in Galatians 3:29 explains how we can receive God's favor through faith in Jesus: *"And if ye be Christ's, then are ye Abraham's seed, and heirs according to the promise."* Have you accepted Jesus as your Lord and Savior? Since we all have been positioned in Christ, every one of us can use our faith to acquire the blessings and wealth promised in Deuteronomy 28. Remember, Jesus is our righteousness and our perfect obedience.

God Favors Abraham

Abraham and his parents, together with all the surrounding people were idol worshippers. However, God has stated in Ephesians 4:18 that people are alienated from Him because of ignorance.

Therefore, when God called Abraham and explained to him about all the favors he would enjoy, Abraham eagerly responded. God's call to Abraham and his response is described in Genesis 12:1-4:

> *Now the LORD had said unto Abram, Get thee out of thy country, and from thy kindred, and from thy father's house, unto a land that I will shew thee: And I will make of thee a great nation, and I will bless thee, and make thy name great; and thou shalt be a blessing: And I will bless them that bless thee, and curse him that curseth thee: and in thee shall all families of the earth be blessed. So Abraham departed, as the LORD had spoken unto him; and Lot went with him: and Abraham was seventy and five years old when he departed out of Haran.*

God indeed blessed Abraham and protected his family. When they went down to Egypt, Pharaoh took Sarah away from Abraham and placed her in his palace to become one of his wives with the understanding that Sarah was Abraham's sister. Although Abraham and Sarah had lied to Pharaoh, God responded on Abraham's behalf according to Genesis 12:17,18,20:

> *And the LORD plagued Pharaoh and his house with great plagues because of Sarai Abram's wife. And Pharaoh called Abram, and said, What is this that thou hast done unto me? Why didst thou not tell me that she was thy wife? And Pharaoh commanded his men concerning him: and they sent him away, and his wife, and all that he had.*

Pharaoh understood that Abraham had the favor of God. He became afraid of Abraham and became more comfortable when Abraham left the area.

God's favor on Abraham was displayed in the incident when Lot his nephew was captured by an army that fought against the king of Sodom. Genesis 14:14,15 provide some details:

> *And when Abram heard that his brother was taken captive, he armed his trained servants, born in his own house, three hundred and eighteen, and pursued them unto Dan. And he divided himself against them, he and his servants, by night, and smote them, and pursued them unto Hobah, which is on the left hand of Damascus. And he brought back all the goods, and also brought again his brother Lot, and his goods, and the women also, and the people.*

Concerning wealth, God had blessed Abraham with more than enough. He possessed so much wealth that Genesis 13: 2 declares, *"And Abram was very rich in cattle, in silver, and in gold."*

Abraham saw many years go by without having an heir. However, God has His timing planned. Genesis 21:1-3 declares: *"And the LORD visited Sarah as he had said, and the LORD did unto Sarah as he had spoken. For Sarah conceived, and bare Abraham a son in his old age, at the set time of which God had spoken to him."*

Just because the Divine favor God promised us seems delayed, does not mean it will not come. If it tarries, wait for it. What God promises will always take place.

David Experienced God's Favor

There is no doubt that God gave preferential treatment to David. When he was just a teenager, God chose him among all his brothers to become king of Israel. We recall that the prophet Samuel thought that God had chosen the tall, handsome Eliab to be the new king of Israel. He was mistaken according to 1 Samuel 16:6,7: *"And it came to pass, when they were come, that he looked on Eliab, and said, Surely the LORD's anointed is before him. But the LORD said unto Samuel, Look not on his countenance, or on the height of his stature; because I have refused him: for the LORD seeth not as man seeth; for man looketh on the outward appearance, but the LORD looketh on the heart."*

When David, who was in the field tending the sheep, was sent for, and came in, God said to Samuel in 1 Samuel 16:12 (last part): *". . . Arise, anoint him: for this is he."*

The Almighty God made a decision to send His Son, our Savior, Jesus, through the lineage of David and to set up an earthly kingdom on David's throne according to Isaiah 9:7: *"Of the increase of his government and peace there shall be no end, upon the throne of David, and upon his kingdom, to order it, and to establish it with judgment and with justice from henceforth even for ever."*

God showed such favor upon David that his son, Solomon, was also exceedingly blessed. Solomon had peace throughout his reign and enormous wealth. Solomon's wealth is described in 1 Kings 10:14,15,22 (NLT):

> *Each year Solomon received about 25 tons of gold. This did not include the additional revenue he received from merchants and traders, all the kings of Arabia, and the governors of the land. The king had a fleet of trading ships that sailed with Hiram's fleet. Once every three years the ships returned, loaded with gold, silver, ivory, apes, and peacocks.*

God's Favor On Mary The Mother Of Jesus

A common, unassuming, humble teenager was chosen and called to be the mother of the Son of God. She was given the responsibility of nurturing, and training the most powerful miracle worker, the most powerful man the world has ever known. Luke 1:26-28 declares the meeting between the angel Gabriel and Mary *"In the sixth month of Elizabeth's pregnancy, God sent the angel Gabriel to Nazareth, a village in Galilee, to a virgin named*

Mary. She was engaged to be married to a man named Joseph, a descendant of king David. Gabriel appeared to her and said, "Greetings, favored woman! The Lord is with you!"

Mary was not merely surprised but confused by the words of the angel. Then she became even more surprised as she learned of her new role and responsibility according to Luke 1:29-32:

> *Confused and disturbed, Mary tried to think what the angel could mean. "Don't be afraid, Mary," the angel told her, "for you have found favor with God! You will conceive and give birth to a son, and you will name him Jesus. He will be very great and will be called the son of the Most High. The Lord God will give him the throne of his ancestor David. And he will reign over Israel forever; his kingdom will never end!*

It is this same Jesus, born of Mary, but conceived by the Holy Ghost: It is this same Jesus through whom every one of us is awarded Divine favor. Remember, that faith in Jesus provides great favor with God.

In conclusion, we have studied how Abraham, David, Solomon and Mary were fortunate to find favor with God. Every one of us has also found favor with God. Jesus has satisfied the obedience requirement for each one of us. Let us therefore constantly claim Divine favor. Every day we have opportunities to exercise our faith and receive all the blessings mentioned in the twenty-eight chapter of Deuteronomy. If you have the faith to believe and receive God's free gifts, tell Him you love Him and tell Him you are thankful for the protection, the riches, and honor with which you have been blessed.

CHAPTER 20

I Am More Than A Conqueror

Although this earth has been a dangerous war zone for more than 6000 years, most of us are surprised or even shocked when we encounter war casualties. In fact, when we are personally affected, our first question is, why me? This sermon is geared to make us more sensitive to the fact that whether we like it or not, we have been thrust into serious warfare against vicious, unrelenting forces of evil. We must become aware, therefore, that every one of us is a soldier. The critical and troubling question is, are we prepared for the war that surrounds us and involves us, or are we blissfully asleep? Perhaps, as many as 90 % of Christians are unaware that a serious, destructive war is taking place in our world, in our environment, right in our own homes.

The reality that the war exists is revealed in Revelation 12:12 (NKJ): *"Therefore rejoice, O heavens, and you who dwell in them! Woe to the inhabitants of the earth and the sea! For the devil has come down to you, having great wrath, because he knows that he has a short time."*

Jesus supports the reality of the dangers of this earth with these words found in John 10:10: *"The thief cometh not, but for to steal, and to kill, and to destroy: I am come that they might have life, and that they might have it more abundantly."*

It is in the context of human ignorance and apathy towards the war that the Apostle Paul advises us in Ephesians 6:10-12:

> *Finally, my brethren, be strong in the Lord, and in the power of his might. Put on the whole armour of God, that ye may be able to stand against the wiles of the devil. For we wrestle not gainst flesh and blood, but against principalities against powers, against the rulers of the darkness of this world, against spiritual wickedness in high places.*

Note well that the Apostle Paul advises us to be strong in the Lord. We dare not attempt to fight in our own strength. Why can't we defeat the enemy in our own strength? We will fail because human strength can never overcome unseen principalities and powers. To overcome, we need to be strong in the Lord and in the power of His might. When we go to battle in our own strength, it is like attempting to fight tanks and sophisticated weapons with bow and arrows.

When the Spanish conquistadores with their guns confronted the native Indians in Mexico and Peru, it was a disaster for those natives. Spain took over Mexico and Peru and that is why the modern people of Mexico and Peru today speak Spanish.

The Weapons of Our Warfare

In 2 Corinthians 10:3, 4, the Apostle Paul describes the effectiveness of the weapons used by believers who are in Christ: *"For though we walk in the flesh, we do not war after the flesh: (For the weapons of our warfare are not carnal, but mighty through God to the pulling down of strongholds;)"*

It is God, Himself, who operates through Christians. Therefore, because we are instruments in the hands of God, we are more than conquerors according to Romans 8:37: *"Nay, in all these things we are more than conquerors through him that loved us."*

The weapons that a true Christian employs are given in detail in Ephesians 6:13-16:
Wherefore take unto you the whole armour of God, that ye may be able to withstand in the evil day, and having done all, to stand. Stand therefore, having your loins girt about with truth, and having on the breastplate of righteousness; And your feet shod with the preparation of the gospel of peace; Above all, taking the shield of faith, wherewith ye shall be able to quench all the fiery darts of the wicked. And taking the helmet of salvation, and the sword of the Spirit, which is the word of God:

All six pieces of the armor are important, because without any one of them, the follower of the Lord becomes vulnerable or easily hurt. Therefore, we must pour God's truth into our hearts daily feasting on the word of God.

In the absence of Christ's righteousness, we have on filthy rags and cannot stand in the presence of God. We need to remember that righteousness is like a garment that we put on by faith.

Moreover, the shield of faith defends us against the fiery darts of the enemy. Faith comes from hearing the word of God. The Bible teaches that without faith it is impossible to please God.

Our feet need the gospel of peace in order to be protected. The gospel brings the good news and provides hope. When we hear the good news, our faith is ignited.

Since our head is so important, it needs to be protected at all times. The helmet of salvation protects the head. It is the knowledge and assurance that we have been saved. Remember 2 Timothy 1:9 declares that God saved us before the world began.

The most aggressive part of our armor is the sword of the Spirit, which is the word of God. According to Hebrews 4:12, the word of God is sharper than a two edged sword.

Soldiers Must Be Alert

In Ephesians 5:14, we read: *"Wherefore he saith, Awake thou that sleepest, and arise from the dead, and Christ shall give thee light."*

Additionally, Romans 13:11,12 encourages us to be on the alert because of limited time that is at our disposal:

> *And that, knowing the time, that now it is high time to awake out of sleep: for now is our salvation nearer than when we believed. The night is far spent, the day is at hand: let us therefore cast off the works of darkness, and let us put on the armour of light.*

The Need For Fasting And Prayer

The Bible contains several examples of the effectiveness of fasting and prayer. We recall in 2 Chronicles 20 how Jehoshaphat, King of Judah, mobilized all his people to gather together to pray and fast, when they were threatened by the combined armies of Moab and the Ammonites. 2 Chronicles 20:3 declares: *"And Jehoshaphat feared, and set himself to seek the LORD, and proclaimed a fast throughout all Judah."* We recall that the Lord caused the enemy soldiers to fight and destroy each other and none escaped.

Just before Jesus began His public ministry, He fasted and prayed for forty days and forty nights. Matthew 4:1,2 state: *"Then was Jesus led up of the spirit into the wilderness to be tempted of the devil. And when he had fasted forty days and forty nights, he was afterward an hungred.*" Of course we know that Jesus accomplished His mission successfully.

Fasting and prayer prepare us for battle. During the period of the Early Church in the Book of Acts, every time they chose men and women to send out to battle, they fasted and prayed.

In conclusion, let us avoid complacency. Let us remember that we are on the battlefield. We must be alert and must be constantly praying according to Ephesians 6:18: *"Praying always with all prayer and supplication in the Spirit, and watching thereunto with all perseverance and supplication for all saints;"*

CPSIA information can be obtained
at www.ICGtesting.com
Printed in the USA
BVHW040014020323
659478BV00005B/458

9 781477 145081